"This is the best book I have read on Dietrich Bonhoeffer the theological educator. Against great odds in the time of Nazi terror, Bonhoeffer forged a distinctive pattern of preparing faithful ministers of the gospel for the service of the church. Paul House argues convincingly that those engaged in the same work today have much to learn from Bonhoeffer's model."

Timothy George, Founding Dean, Beeson Divinity School; General Editor, Reformation Commentary on Scripture

"In all the writing about Bonhoeffer, few scholars focus on his work as a seminary leader. As a result, we forget that one of his most famous works, *Life Together*, emerged from such a community. Paul House dares to apply this and other Bonhoeffer works to the challenges facing contemporary seminaries. Even those who ultimately disagree with House's argument for life-on-life education will benefit from reading his countercultural critique."

Collin Hansen, Editorial Director, The Gospel Coalition; author, *Blind Spots: Becoming a Courageous C̶* *Commissioned Church*

"While the circumstances B̶ : very different from the challenges faci̶ strates why Bonhoeffer's approach to th̶ ..y remains a model for today's seminary le̶ ...u students. This is a fine, thoughtful study of Bonhoeffer's approach to theological education and its implications for the complex, changing world of seminary education today."

Victoria J. Barnett, General Editor, *Dietrich Bonhoeffer Works*, English edition

"Paul House not only offers a primer on an often-neglected role of Bonhoeffer's life, but also insightfully critiques much of contemporary American higher education—theological or otherwise. Reading this splendid book might not alleviate all the ills of modern higher education, but House certainly leaves educators and administrators with fewer excuses."

Richard A. Bailey, Associate Professor of History, Canisius College; author, *Race and Redemption in Puritan New England*

"The church in North America just passed the sign announcing dangerous rapids ahead. We need strong pulpits. What's more, we need faithful theological training. Paul House draws our attention to the courageous wisdom found in Dietrich Bonhoeffer. We know Bonhoeffer for his classic texts and for his resistance to Hitler. But he also directed a seminary. Listen to Bonhoeffer. He will help us navigate what lies ahead."

Stephen J. Nichols, President, Reformation Bible College; Chief Academic Officer, Ligonier Ministries

"With clarity and verve, Paul House ably demonstrates, synthesizes, and applies Bonhoeffer's historic insights into theological education. The result is a timely and fresh reclamation of our life together for the church and for colleges and seminaries seeking to come alongside the church in discipling future pastors. A must-read for professors, pastors, administrators, and students who want to know the what, why, and how of theological education."

Christopher W. Morgan, Dean and Professor of Theology, California Baptist University

"Bonhoeffer's prescription for seminary training should only be followed if we want to see a generation of ministers characterized by faithfulness, courage, and community. Otherwise, we can continue in the same path we're on, where pastors learn to be entertainers, life-coaches, and pop-psychologists. Thank God that during this current revival of interest in Bonhoeffer, Paul House had the wisdom to focus on what Bonhoeffer knew best and did so very well."

C. Ben Mitchell, Provost and Vice President for Academic Affairs and Graves Professor of Moral Philosophy, Union University

Bonhoeffer's Seminary Vision

BONHOEFFER'S SEMINARY VISION

A Case for Costly Discipleship and Life Together

PAUL R. HOUSE

CROSSWAY

WHEATON, ILLINOIS

Published by Crossway
 1300 Crescent Street
 Wheaton, Illinois 60187

Cover design: Dual Identity, inc.

Cover image: © iStock

First printing 2015

Printed in the United States of America

Trade paperback ISBN: 978-1-4335-4544-3
ePub ISBN: 978-1-4335-4547-4
PDF ISBN: 978-1-4335-4545-0
Mobipocket ISBN: 978-1-4335-4546-7

Library of Congress Cataloging-in-Publication Data

House, Paul R., 1958–
  Bonhoeffer's seminary vision: a case for costly discipleship and life together / Paul R. House.
    pages cm
  Includes bibliographical references and indexes.
  ISBN 978-1-4335-4544-3 (tp)
  1. Bonhoeffer, Dietrich, 1906–1945. 2. Clergy—Training of. 3. Theology—Study and teaching. 4. Pastoral theology. I. Title.
  BX4827.B57H685   2015
  230.071'1—dc23   2014030581

Crossway is a publishing ministry of Good News Publishers.

VP		25	24	23	22	21	20	19	18	17	16	15
15	14	13	12	11	10	9	8	7	6	5	4	3	2	1

To Heather

Contents

Preface

My interest in Dietrich Bonhoeffer and in personal, incarnational education began in the late 1970s. Like many others of my generation, I first encountered his writings as a college student. During my final undergraduate semester I took an independent study course entitled Classics of Christian Devotion under the tutelage of Tom Padgett, the chair of our English department. Padgett assigned me works by Bunyan, Milton, and Dante. He also asked me to read Bonhoeffer's *The Cost of Discipleship*, and even gave me a pocket-sized edition containing his own marginal notes, a volume I still cherish. At the time, the main impact *The Cost of Discipleship* had on me was to challenge me to think harder about what it means to be a Christian. Bonhoeffer's life story, as told in the introduction to the edition I had, also illustrated to me an exemplary Christian life. Padgett's example was even more important to me than the assigned reading since he showed me how incarnational Christian educators engage students. He remains one of my main models as I pursue the teaching craft.

After taking an MA in English, I began seminary studies. My seminary had three thousand students. The teachers were excellent lecturers, which was important given the generally large sections they taught. But they turned over all grading and general course administration to doctoral students and, despite being generally approachable, did not always seek to spend time with students. The numbers certainly made such personal contact difficult, though not impossible.

In my last year, I took a course in twentieth-century European church history, led by Penrose St. Amant, who had studied in Edinburgh and taught in Switzerland. There were ten of us in the course, the smallest class I attended during seminary. St. Amant assigned me a paper surveying Bonhoeffer's writings, so I read *Creation and Fall*, *Temptation*, the then most recent edition of *Letters and Papers from Prison*, *Life Together*, *The Cost of Discipleship*, and the first edition of Eberhard Bethge's biography, among other things. I recall St. Amant asking me to please figure out what "religionless Christianity" meant. I was not very helpful on that issue, but my Bonhoeffer reading expanded.

St. Amant also took a personal interest in me and in Jim Dixon, a close friend of mine who was in the same course. On one memorable evening Dr. and Mrs. St. Amant took our wives and us to one of the best restaurants in the city, certainly the best one I went to while a student. After the waiter brought the women roses at the end of the evening, I asked to help with the check. He replied, "Don't worry about this, House. I am very wealthy." I learned from another professor that the St. Amants were indeed moneyed people. He taught because he felt called to and liked doing so, and because he enjoyed spending time with interested students. Like Padgett, he was an educator in the incarnational mold.

When I became a college teacher, I kept reading Bonhoeffer's works. I assigned *The Cost of Discipleship* in New Testament survey classes and recommended *Creation and Fall* in Pentateuch courses. In my first ten years in teaching, I served an institution deeply involved in shaping students. Over the years I was able to baptize, counsel, discipline, marry, and even help bury some of our students. Yet it was also at that institution that I first encountered nonembodied, impersonal extension work and the largely financial arguments for offering it. Church work expanded my efforts to care about people in a local context. Bonhoeffer's *Sanctorum Communio* and *Act and Being* were particularly helpful as I tried to integrate faith, learning, and service of the church. During these years I supplemented what I had learned from Bethge's biography with other good treatments of Bonhoeffer's life.

Since those first ten years, I have been involved in seminary teaching fourteen of the last seventeen years. One seminary I served was large and not particularly personal. While there I tried very hard to invest in students that I could get to know. The seminary had no structural intentionality that helped this effort. The other two seminaries I have served, including Beeson Divinity School of Samford University, where I now teach, are smaller and intentionally personal in purpose and practice, though the first of these was instituting online classes. Through these places and through visiting and teaching at comparable ones in Europe, Australia, and Asia I think I have come to understand better what Bonhoeffer describes in *Life Together*.

For six years I supervised academic affairs, admissions, and student life at Beeson, which helped me gain perspective on how the parts of a seminary fit together. To try to do my work better I read several histories of individual seminaries and about thirty biographies of persons involved in seminary work. I strived to formulate a more thoroughly theological understanding of how seminary work ought to operate. Regular talks with my supervisor and dean, Timothy George, included the biblical-theological basis of what we were trying to do with our students, staff, and faculty. As part of this quest I examined Bonhoeffer's seminary work more closely, particularly through the growing number of volumes in the *Dietrich Bonhoeffer Works* and the new (and even larger) edition of Bethge's biography.

The Hodges Chapel at Beeson is a marvel in many ways, not the least of which is the way it depicts the global scope of the gospel and the human price that has been paid for its extension. For instance, it houses six busts of martyrs, one from each inhabited continent. Bonhoeffer represents Europe. For this and other reasons Dean George fairly regularly focuses our community's attention on Bonhoeffer and the era in which he lived. For example, in 2012 we had a special spring semester emphasis on Bonhoeffer, which was preceded two years earlier by a series on the Barmen Declaration. It seems natural for me, then, to consider Bonhoeffer's views on seminary education in our setting.

It also seems natural to think about personal, incarnational education because of the nature of Beeson itself. Established in 1988, it determined to limit enrollment to 180 students from the outset and to give these students personal attention and intentional shaping for ministry. A good endowment helps realize this vision, but so does ongoing support, long-term leadership, a carefully chosen and dedicated faculty, teachable students, fiscal responsibility, a home at a university, and self-control that makes adding programs, buildings, and other earmarks of personal agendas unimportant. People can and do matter at such a place.

Over the past twenty years all of us in seminary education have increasingly encountered new technology delivery systems. At first the goal was to use these to enhance courses offered on campus. Then classes began to be offered online, as they had been in old-style correspondence courses. I have seen the tide gradually shift from seminaries having to give a reason to administrators, constituents, and accrediting agencies for offering online courses to giving a reason for not doing so. As church contributions have waned and costs risen, I have seen seminaries look longingly to the web to solve their financial troubles. However, when I have queried others about the theological basis for online education, I have usually gotten blank stares or some statement about how technology is the future and will help seminaries balance their budgets. Once or twice someone has used the Bible's epistles or a rather broad definition of "missions" as a theological rationale for various forms of electronic courses for credit. Speaking to me confidentially, some academic deans have said that they and their seminaries' teachers do not prefer online classes to in-person ones, yet have come to accept online courses as a necessary evil of sorts. Several professors have conveyed the same sentiments to me. However, I have also met many administrators and teachers who take on this task with goodwill and hopefulness. It did not surprise me, then, when a few years ago degrees offered completely through electronic means were accredited.

Our seminary has not offered online courses and currently does not plan to do so, which has made us somewhat unusual in our guild. I have taken this changing situation in seminary education as more incentive to continue working toward a clearer theology of seminary education. I have sought to discern what makes education offered face-to-face, electronically, or through a blended version of the two more or less biblical, and I have continued to seek the best way to express a theological basis for the sort of personal education that impacted me.

As I considered these issues, it occurred to me that Bonhoeffer was a seminary director and teacher for a very eventful five years. Some of his most influential books emerged out of and were about seminary theory and practice. So I have turned to his writings once again, this time to try to discern his theology of seminary ministry and to consider if or how to apply his theology and practice to our current situation.

As this book will show, I find that his biblical analysis makes it inescapable to link seminary education, and all fully Christian ministries, to the New Testament's incarnation principle of the body of Christ, which fits the Old Testament's presentation of all sorts of education as a face-to-face intergenerational enterprise. Thus, I believe that a biblical theology of pastoral formation makes face-to-face community-based seminary education a priority, not a preference. (I also believe that the same is true of a Christian liberal arts university, but that is a subject for another time.) Online education for degree credit (at per-credit fees) may be reserved for true emergency cases, but must not be accepted as normative or used regularly for pastoral formation. Focusing on this incarnational priority will help us find solutions to the problems we face or lead to new patterns altogether. Regardless, it will not leave us drifting toward practices that are not inevitable unless we allow them to be.

I am not a Bonhoeffer specialist. I am an Old Testament theologian who has spent a few decades in the church, in the university, in the Scriptures, in the seminary, and in Bonhoeffer's works. Based on my training in historical and exegetical studies I have tried to do viable work by offering close readings of primary sources and a faithful exposition of their historical setting such as I would try to do when interpreting Old Testament texts. I am not a Bonhoeffer hagiographer; he was a man with flaws, as he well knew. In short, I am a Bonhoeffer reader seeking biblical-theological understanding of my vocation for the sake of the church, the body of Christ. I am grateful to the people who have written about Bonhoeffer, translated his works, and kept his example of personal education alive. Their labors have enriched my life. Bonhoeffer might not agree with my interpretation of his works in this book, but I am quite certain he would think I am right about one thing: we must think theologically, not just pragmatically, about the training of pastors, a task he described in 1942 as "worthy of our ultimate commitment."

Acknowledgments

Memory and gratitude are among God's finest gifts, particularly when experienced together. Writing this book provided me many such moments. It gave me the privilege of remembering Dietrich Bonhoeffer, Eberhard Bethge, and their lesser-known faithful colleague Fritz Onnasch. It reminded me I could only do so because Victoria J. Barnett, H. Gaylon Barker, Mark S. Brocker, and other scholars have made essential material on Bonhoeffer's seminary ministry accessible. It also occasioned memories of my teachers, living and dead, who gave me mannerisms, ideas, and practices I use daily. They showed me why the quality, content, *and* form of education matter. Thus, I am grateful for Minnie Weems, Kenneth Shippy, Larry Hymer, Burney Johnson, Don Johnston, Don Bogle, Gerald Cowen, Tom Padgett, Betty Gipson, Penrose St. Amant, and John D. W. Watts. I am also accountable to them.

Other memories also spark deep gratitude. Beeson Divinity School of Samford University provided faculty development funds, a working model of life-on-life pastoral formation, and a collegial environment in which to work. Dean Timothy George, Associate Dean David Hogg, and former Associate Dean Burch Barger encouraged me in different, and essential, ways. Justin Taylor, Thom Notaro, Erik Maldre, Amy Kruis, and Angie Cheatham at Crossway were helpful at every appropriate stage. Michael Moore of Fortress Press was generous when granting permission to quote from *Dietrich Bonhoeffer's Works*, volumes 9–16, and helped me secure rights from other publishers. Wendell Berry's essays, novels, poems, and example offered consistent direction, discipline, and hope. Gene Logsdon's essays and novels made me think more seriously about people and about theological education. My friends Tom Jones, Richard Bailey, Ben Mitchell, Greg Thornbury, Don West, Chase Kuhn, Grant Taylor, Kyle McClellan, James Dixon, and Scott Hafemann gave me needed advice and laughter.

Family members provided other essential physical and spiritual resources. David and Dawn Oldfield, my wife's parents, contributed a quiet rural home in which to write, memorable family gatherings, and a living example of commitment to a community. Gordon and Suzanne Kingsley, my brother-in-law and sister, completed their long service in higher education and thus modeled perseverance and hope. My parents, Roy and Lee House, continued to take interest in my writing and to provide an example of Christian people working productively long after it is convenient. My daughter, Molly Spence, her husband, Martin, and their son, Caleb, gave their love and reminded me that future generations need personal, local, and communal pastoral formation.

Most importantly, my wife, Heather, provided love, home, hope, a listening ear for my various rants, and a cautioning voice about reading depressing material late at night. I dedicate this book to her with gratitude for our shared life and the memories we are making.

Abbreviations

Bethge, *DB*   Eberhard Bethge. *Dietrich Bonhoeffer: A Biography.*
                    Rev. ed. Edited by Victoria J. Barnett. Translated by Eric
                    Mosbacher, Peter Ross, Betty Ross, Frank Clarke, and
                    William Glen-Doepel. Minneapolis: Augsburg Fortress,
                    2000.

DBW   *Dietrich Bonhoeffer Works.* 16 vols. Minneapolis: For-
                    tress, 1996–2013. Translated from *Dietrich Bonhoef-
                    fer Werke*. Edited by Eberhard Bethge et al. Munich:
                    Christian Kaiser, 1986–1999.

DBW 1   Vol. 1, *Sanctorum Communio: A Theological Study
                    of the Sociology of the Church*. Edited by Clifford J.
                    Green. Translated by Reinhard Krauss and Nancy
                    Lukens.

DBW 2   Vol. 2, *Act and Being: Transcendental Philosophy
                    and Ontology in Systematic Theology*. Edited by
                    Wayne Whitson Floyd Jr. Translated by H. Martin
                    Rumscheidt.

DBW 3   Vol. 3, *Creation and Fall: A Theological Exposition of
                    Genesis 1–3*. Edited by John W. de Gruchy. Translated
                    by Douglas Stephen Bax.

DBW 4   Vol. 4, *Discipleship*. Edited by Geffrey B. Kelly and
                    John D. Godsey. Translated by Barbara Green and
                    Reinhard Krauss.

DBW 5   Vol. 5, *Life Together* and *Prayerbook of the Bible*.
                    Edited by Geffrey B. Kelly. Translated by Daniel W.
                    Bloesch and James H. Burtness.

DBW 11	Vol. 11, *Ecumenical, Academic, and Pastoral Work: 1931–1932*. Edited by Victoria J. Barnett, Mark S. Brocker, and Michael B. Lukens. Translated by Anne Schmidt-Lange, with Isabel Best, Nicholas Humphrey, and Marion Pauck. Supplementary material translated by Douglas W. Stott.
DBW 12	Vol. 12, *Berlin: 1932–1933*. Edited by Larry L. Rasmussen. Translated by Isabel Best and David Higgins. Supplementary material translated by Douglas W. Stott.
DBW 13	Vol. 13, *London: 1933–1935*. Edited by Keith Clements. Translated by Isabel Best. Supplementary material translated by Douglas W. Stott.
DBW 14	Vol. 14, *Theological Education at Finkenwalde: 1935–1937*. Edited by H. Gaylon Barker and Mark S. Brocker. Translated by Douglas W. Stott.
DBW 15	Vol. 15, *Theological Education Underground: 1937–1940*. Edited by Victoria J. Barnett. Translated by Victoria J. Barnett, Claudia D. Bergmann, Peter Frick, and Scott A. Moore. Supplementary material translated by Douglas W. Stott.
DBW 16	Vol. 16, *Conspiracy and Imprisonment: 1940–1945*. Edited by Mark S. Brocker. Translated by Lisa E. Dahill. Supplementary material translated by Douglas W. Stott.
de Gruchy, *EB*	John W. de Gruchy. *Daring, Trusting Spirit: Bonhoeffer's Friend Eberhard Bethge*. Minneapolis: Fortress, 2005.
Schlingensiepen, *DB*	Ferdinand Schlingensiepen. *Dietrich Bonhoeffer 1906–1945: Martyr, Thinker, Man of Resistance*. Translated by Isabel Best. London: T&T Clark, 2012.

1

Bonhoeffer's Path to Seminary Ministry

The matter of the proper education of preachers of the gospel is worthy of our ultimate commitment.

Dietrich Bonhoeffer (1942)

Introduction

Dietrich Bonhoeffer was a seminary director and teacher for five years (1935–1940), longer than he served consecutively in any other job. This work provided the context for some of his best and best-known writings, for meeting several key persons, and for making some of his most significant decisions. It seems logical to conclude, then, that understanding Bonhoeffer requires some particular focus on his theology and practice of pastoral formation in a seminary context. Yet Bonhoeffer's biographers and scholars writing about him rarely highlight this aspect of his life and writing. They usually emphasize his roles as pastor, ecumenist, theologian, and Resistance member.

This tendency likely stems from the fact that these are the elements of Bonhoeffer's life his close friend and literary executor Eberhard Bethge stressed in his editing of Bonhoeffer's unpublished writings and in his magisterial essential biography of Bonhoeffer published in 1967 and revised in 1989 (English revised edition 2000).[1] Bethge had good reasons for his choices. Bonhoeffer was not a hero in Germany immediately after World War II, even in some church circles. Many Germans thought he died as a political prisoner, perhaps even a treasonous one, not as a martyr of the faith.[2] Bethge could also see that Bonhoeffer's writings might eventually be forgotten. Thus, it was natural and right for him to stress his close friend's theology and describe how it led Bonhoeffer to take actions that ultimately resulted in his execution. Bethge's narrative is certainly defensible. Despite its length, it is also brisk and often quite moving.

Subsequent biographers and commentators have understandably followed Bethge's lead. After all, he knew his subject extremely well and had access to family records, in part because he married Bonhoeffer's niece Renate, who aided and participated in his historical research.[3] Furthermore, as John de Gruchy, Bethge's biographer, demonstrates, Bethge was a tireless and accurate historian.[4] Bethge did not just draw on his own and other eyewitness memories and Bonhoeffer's published works. He recovered and utilized reams of documentary material. Indeed it was largely due to Bethge's exhaustive and efficient efforts to preserve items written by and to Bonhoeffer that the *Dietrich Bonhoeffer Works*[5] series numbers sixteen volumes. Bonhoeffer studies as we know them would not exist without Bethge.

Interestingly, de Gruchy also observes that Bethge does not always mention the full extent of his own part in some of Bon-

---

[1] Eberhard Bethge, *Dietrich Bonhoeffer: A Biography*, rev. ed., ed. Victoria J. Barnett, trans. Eric Mosbacher et al. (Minneapolis: Augsburg Fortress, 2000); hereafter Bethge, *DB*.

[2] This concern to emphasize the connection between Bonhoeffer's imprisonment and his Christian faith is evident in the title of the first American edition of one of Bonhoeffer's most studied books, *Prisoner for God: Letters and Papers from Prison*, ed. Eberhard Bethge, trans. Reginald H. Fuller (New York: Macmillan, 1954). Subsequent editions dropped the first part of the title.

[3] See, for instance, her *Dietrich Bonhoeffer: A Brief Life*, trans. K. C. Hanson (Minneapolis: Augsburg Fortress, 2004); and Eberhard Bethge and Renate Bethge, eds., *Last Letters of Resistance: Farewells from the Bonhoeffer Family*, trans. Dennis Slabaugh (Philadelphia: Fortress, 1986).

[4] John W. de Gruchy, *Daring, Trusting Spirit: Bonhoeffer's Friend Eberhard Bethge* (Minneapolis: Fortress, 2005), 112–44, 151–57, 176–94; hereafter de Gruchy, *EB*.

[5] See the table of abbreviations for German and English editions, including individual English volumes. Unless otherwise noted, all citations are from the English edition, abbreviated as *DBW*.

hoeffer's activities. He keeps himself in the background as much as possible as he tells Bonhoeffer's story. For instance, Bethge discloses conversations he observed Bonhoeffer have with others without noting he was an eyewitness.[6] Bethge clearly wishes to introduce and validate his friend. He does not write to preserve his own legacy in the Bonhoeffer story.

Though admirable, Bethge's humility about his shared work with Bonhoeffer may result in his readers' missing Bonhoeffer's ongoing significance as a theological educator and Bethge's important collaboration in that era of Bonhoeffer's life. Bethge was part of Bonhoeffer's seminary ministry from the beginning. He was a student in the first class Bonhoeffer led as director in 1935, and afterward was Bonhoeffer's indispensable associate director until the Gestapo closed the seminaries in 1940. Bethge certainly recounts this phase of Bonhoeffer's life. But it seems to me he does so always with an eye on Bonhoeffer's continuing role in the Confessing Church and his gradual decision to enter the Resistance. The seminary work stays in the background along with Bethge.

It is also possible that Bethge does not highlight Bonhoeffer's (and his own) efforts in seminary work more fully because one could assume certain things about seminary education in those days. First, it occurred in a face-to-face, personal setting. Second, the students were generally men[7] who had studied theology at a university and taken the first of two ordination exams. Third, the students received standard instruction in selected practical disciplines. Fourth, seminary studies were a capstone experience. They took place at the end of the educational experience and over a short period of time, only six months or so. Fifth, there is some monotony in the tasks associated with receiving and sending out seminarians over and over again. Bethge may have given the subject as much attention as he thought interesting to readers, or found interesting himself. Sixth, and perhaps most tellingly for our day, Bethge could

---

[6] See de Gruchy, *EB*, 153–54.
[7] Bonhoeffer had female students while teaching at the University of Berlin, but all his seminarians were male.

not have predicted how unusual Bonhoeffer's approach to personal theological education would become.

Other Bonhoeffer scholars have not dealt with this portion of Bonhoeffer's life for other reasons. Jürgen Henkys observes:

> No period of Bonhoeffer's life and work seems more inaccessible today or more inclined to put people off than does the Finkenwalde period. Indeed, in many readers it generates genuine opposition. The academic, ecumenical, political Bonhoeffer presents a more welcoming figure to many who turn to his work than does the Bonhoeffer . . . who was confrontational and demanding in ecclesiastical matters, radically biblical, and rigorous in matters of piety.[8]

Today we can add to that list the Bonhoeffer who put so much emphasis on theological education in a personal, communal setting. Henkys adds that the trajectory of German seminary life after World War II also leads Bonhoeffer experts away from analyzing his seminary work. Seminaries in West Germany became interested in "asserting their own status and mission within the larger framework of the official college and university system," while seminaries in East Germany ceased to operate or were incorporated into universities.[9] Thus, Bonhoeffer's seminaries have been considered simply part of a historical era instead of a direct ancestor of what remains a living witness.

These reservations are understandable, but they are not decisive. Bonhoeffer's time as seminary director deserves further specific analysis, for at least three reasons. First, by any measure it was a crucial era in his life. In fact, Bethge noted in 1954, "It was in this task that Bonhoeffer's theological and personal influence was at its greatest."[10] Second, those who wish to understand Bonhoeffer as theologian and activist may wish to consider how he integrated those tasks in his seminary work. In an essay arguing for Bonhoef-

---

[8] Jürgen Henkys, "Editor's Afterword to the German Edition" (*Dietrich Bonhoeffer Werke*), in *DBW* 14:971–72.
[9] Ibid., 1013–14.
[10] See Bonhoeffer, *Prisoner for God*, 8.

fer's desire to be "with" and "for" others, Samuel Wells concludes, "In this sense, Bonhoeffer's most radical step was to become an educator. In setting up the seminary at Finkenwalde, Bonhoeffer trained students . . . to learn to do what they could do for themselves."[11] He then adds, "In *Life Together*, Bonhoeffer's whole attention is upon the challenge, gift, imperative, and grace of 'being with' one another. In that sense . . . we can see *Life Together* as the book that sums up Bonhoeffer's theology as well as his own life."[12] Third, current events warrant seeking resources for the renewal of theological education. Thus, closer attention to Bonhoeffer's time in seminary directorship may well help us, as Henkys puts it, "find unfinished business in what might initially seem rather alien to us, or to be motivated by something quite apart from the usual list of fashionable issues."[13]

His Most Radical Step: The Importance of Seminary Ministry in Bonhoeffer's Life

While instructing and directing seminarians Bonhoeffer published what are certainly among his most influential works, *The Cost of Discipleship* (1937) and *Life Together* (1939). He also delivered talks at a 1938 retreat of former students that were published in English as *Temptation*, gave a significant lecture on faithful endurance to Confessing Church pastors, published meditations on various passages, and composed meditations on Psalm 119:1–21. He developed the framework for *Psalms: Prayerbook of the Bible* (1940), which appeared after his seminary ministry ended. He made his now famous decision to return to Germany from the United States and England on the eve of World War II in 1939. The letters and diary he wrote while in England and the United States indicate that one of the main reasons he returned was to stand with and

---

[11] Samuel Wells, "Bonhoeffer: Theologian, Activist, Educator: Challenges for the Church of the Coming Generation," in *Interpreting Bonhoeffer: Historical Perspectives, Emerging Issues*, ed. Clifford J. Green and Guy C. Carter (Minneapolis: Fortress, 2013), 233–34.
[12] Ibid., 234.
[13] Henkys, "Editor's Afterword to the German Edition," 1014.

care for his spiritual brothers by continuing his seminary ministry.[14] He had told his former students in the messages on temptation, in circular letters, and in a public lecture that they should continue to follow God's call in the Confessing Church.[15] How could he do less?

The end of his seminary ministry and other setbacks were factors in Bonhoeffer's joining the Resistance. He was banned from lecturing at universities in August 1936. He was denied a military chaplaincy by February 1940.[16] The government closed down his last seminary site in March 1940. In September 1940 he was banned from speaking in public, and in March 1941 banned from publishing. Most of his former and prospective students were drafted into the German military by 1940, and some had already been killed in action. His public ministry options were almost down to zero, and he did not wish to be a regular soldier in the German army for several reasons. Thus, he had few options, a point that needs to be recalled when analyzing why he took the steps he did afterward. He became a member of the German secret service by 1940 and was involved with a Resistance group until his arrest in 1943.

Some Unfinished Business: The Importance of Bonhoeffer's Seminary Ministry for Today

Clearly, there are historical reasons to examine Bonhoeffer's seminary ministry. But there are other reasons too. Through his writings from these years he left rich resources for all of us involved in "seminary education," a term I use in this book to include any institution preparing persons specifically for pastoral ministry. These works provide a theological basis for seminary education as a ministry of the visible body of Christ. They portray a seminary as a community of faith and state how that community may live for Christ and for one another. They offer encouragement to former students who have entered the sometimes-harsh world of church ministry. His example from this era demonstrates the need for sacrificial teacher-

---

[14] See, for example, *DBW* 15:215–26; and de Gruchy, *EB*, 41.

[15] *DBW* 15:386–415, 60–62 and 81–85, and 416–37.

[16] According to a letter sent to his parents dated February 27, 1940. See *DBW* 15:297.

pastors in seminary education, given the inherently personal, incarnational, and visible nature of ministerial preparation. Finally, Bonhoeffer's seminary ministry stresses the importance of educating the next generation of pastors. Bonhoeffer believed the German church's future rested in the quality and commitment of its pastors. He went to great lengths to safeguard this future. Frankly, he could not stem the tide. His efforts to do what was right in the face of what he eventually saw as temporarily impossible odds should hearten those of us who face hardships that pale in contrast to his.

To aid seminary education, it is important to read Bonhoeffer's writings from 1935–1940 in their original historical context. Millions have benefited from reading these books and shorter pieces as general guides for individual and corporate life. These works certainly aid believers and Christian communities of various types in living for Christ and with one another before a watching world. Yet they had a more specific context when they were written, and that context was the life of a director of a seminary and what he hoped this ministry could achieve.

These works were presented to and written about seminary students, seminary supporters, and seminary alumni. Thus, it is right to examine them with that context in mind for our current situation's sake. They will not provide every answer to current problems, and one need not always agree with all Bonhoeffer's theological formulations and ideas about seminaries in that day. Still, some sustained interaction with these writings may help us in an age when theology is regularly replaced by marketing strategies and financial plans, and often by flawed ones at that.

To be even more frank, in my opinion seminary educators desperately need these theological underpinnings and this example of determined personal education today. Financial concerns that have been building for decades have recently been made more acute by dwindling church support for seminary education and by worldwide economic troubles. At the same time, electronic devices have made online credits and degrees that require little or no personal time with teachers or other students feasible. Accreditation policies have adapted to these options because the institutions that constitute the associations and the governments that approve them desire such programs. The seminaries often believe these programs will help their budgets. Government entities want as many credentialed (though not necessarily educated or spiritually formed) persons in the work force as possible. To fuel interest, seminary advertising campaigns use terms like "online community" as if one may have communion without actual physical presence. I recently saw a seminary advertisement that had the audacity to call online degrees "personal" because there could be a voice on the phone, a potential letter in the mail, and a hand to shake on graduation day—surely a minimalist definition if I ever saw one.

It is likely that seminary education has entered a new phase in the United States and elsewhere. The phase of proving that theological traditions of various types can produce a viable academic setting through good faculty credentials and an enduring physical plant has passed. So has the phase of proving that seminaries can govern themselves and set and reach reasonable, assessable goals and objectives. It appears we have now entered a phase that will focus on *the form* of theological education, what more industrially oriented persons call "delivery systems." The biblically based, centuries-old belief that theological education should occur in person through mentors with peers in communities in communal places is no longer necessary for every seminary degree's accreditation. Many educators have expressed to me privately that they think that impersonal education through credit and/or degree-granting online or hybrid means (mostly electronic delivery supplemented by students' having brief times with teachers) is simply inevitable, even if they do not think it is desirable or theologically viable. Thus, many existing seminaries need courage for sustained work and for renewal.

On a more positive note, many seminaries are trying to refresh and continue face-to-face education. Also, I believe that new forms of personal seminaries and related ministries will arise in response to impersonal approaches. Meanwhile, current and hoped-for expansion of Christianity around the world creates the continual need for pastoral formation. Thus, new seminaries will be needed as part of this training. These new seminary expressions will arise in all kinds of cultural settings. It is important, then, to understand the biblical-theological bases on which they should be established.

Bonhoeffer's life and writings can help us ask the right questions about the future of seminary education. It is hard to conceive of a person less likely to accept the notion that current trends are unavoidable or that past practices are inviolable. Rather, his approach to theological education reminds us of the necessity of determining what is right and then following that course of action. His writings remind us that like all Christian work theological education needs grounding in *theology*. We cannot simply accept nontheological means of education as our norm. So he reminds us that the right questions are, What sort of education fits the Bible's vision of ministerial preparation? and What sort of minister does the church need? and What is the right thing to do in complicated times? They are not, How do we give our constituents whatever they want? Or, How do we sell degrees like any other commodity? Or, What brand of education pays well in a hurry? Or, How do we fit into the newest trend of educational technology? Or, How do we survive at all costs?

This book attempts to do two things. First, it tries to examine Bonhoeffer's theology and practice of theological education in their original context. Second, it endeavors to assert the biblical necessity of personal, incarnational, face-to-face education for the health of pastors and churches. To try to achieve these goals I will first sketch briefly how Bonhoeffer became a seminary director and note the settings of Bonhoeffer's seminaries. I will then focus on selected writings from 1935–1940 and on his daily and seasonal work as a seminary director. I will quote generously from Bonhoeffer's works, both because his prose is often so telling and because, though I hope my observations about him and his writings are well founded, they are not infallible. In each chapter I will also analyze selected current methods of theological education and suggest alternatives to simply repeating the past or accepting the next wave of education innovations. Finally, I will discuss some objections to the incarnational imperative and suggest ways Bonhoeffer's views can be implemented today.

Bonhoeffer has been utilized on a number of subjects to good effect. Clearly, this subject was close to his heart. It makes sense, then, to converse with his views to think about how to provide theological education for church renewal. My own reflection on Bonhoeffer's ideas and commitments have led me to conclude that we must take the narrow way of personal, incarnational theological education. We can do no less if we believe the church is the visible body of Christ that follows Jesus on the narrow path of faithfulness in all seasons of life.

2

Bonhoeffer and
His Seminaries

Our situation of course was an unparalleled one, and
equally unparalleled were the scholarly qualifications and
pastoral passion which were united in Bonhoeffer; that is
why Finkenwalde just cannot be imitated. But much of
what was worked out and experienced there might be
of lasting value for our student communities.

Wilhelm Rott (1966)

Introduction

Bonhoeffer engaged in university-based theological education before he began his seminary work. By all accounts he was very effective. He began teaching theology in August 1931 at the University
of Berlin, one of the world's most famous academic institutions.
Lecturers had to draw their audiences. They could not depend on
a curriculum that delivered students to their classes to do that for
them. At the beginning Bonhoeffer had about fifteen students, many
of them quite dedicated. Soon he gained a reputation for stimulating lecturing, and his numbers and notoriety grew.[1] His lectures on

---

[1] For eyewitness descriptions of these days, see Ferdinand Schlingensiepen, *Dietrich Bonhoeffer
1906–1945: Martyr, Thinker, Man of Resistance*, trans. Isabel Best (London: T&T Clark, 2012),

Genesis 1–3 were so popular that his students urged him to publish them. They appeared under the title *Creation and Fall* in 1933.[2] By the summer of 1933 his lectures on christology drew as many as two hundred listeners.[3] It seemed he was on the way to a reasonably notable university career.

On a cold March day in 1940, Bonhoeffer left what turned out to be his last lecture room. It was not one of the well-appointed halls of the University of Berlin. He was banned from lecturing there in 1936. Nor was it a fine venue accommodating the delivery of invited lectures at a foreign university. Wartime travel restrictions kept him from giving, for example, the 1940 Croall Lectures at the University of Edinburgh.[4] Rather, the lecture hall he departed was likely a room in a farmhouse on a rural estate called Sigurdshof in what is now Poland, where Bonhoeffer lived with his students and Eberhard Bethge, his associate director.

Bonhoeffer and Bethge did not choose this location because it was comfortable. The house had no indoor plumbing or electricity. It was, quite simply, nearly all that was available to them. Snowfall was so heavy in the winter of 1939–1940 that occasionally mail could not get through. Decimated by the military draft, imprisonment, and general persecution, student numbers were small. If they were all present, eight men, the entire student body of the seminary, attended Bonhoeffer's final class.

This chapter seeks to give readers a broad perspective on Bonhoeffer's path to seminary ministry and the conditions in which Bonhoeffer labored. It will sketch how and why he became a seminary director, then will introduce very briefly his students, the places the seminary met, the schedule the seminary kept, and the curriculum Bonhoeffer oversaw. These basic details are important for one to begin to appreciate Bonhoeffer's educational accomplishments and to make apt comparisons to today.

97–100; hereafter Schlingensiepen, *DB*. For his challenging and stimulating expectations of his students, see his 1933 essay "What Should a Student of Theology Do Today?," in *DBW* 12:432–35.

[2] See *DBW* 3.

[3] Bethge, *DB*, 219.

[4] See *DBW* 15:257, 267.

Bonhoeffer's Path to Seminary Ministry

As the following brief biographical data demonstrates,[5] Bonhoeffer's path to seminary ministry was not a straight and smooth one. Bonhoeffer was born into a very accomplished family on February 6, 1906. He chose theology as his life's work at an early age, and he wasted no time in gaining the necessary credentials. Following completion of his doctoral dissertation in 1927, he spent most of 1928 as an assistant pastor in Barcelona. In 1930 he finished a second dissertation, which was required for qualification as a university lecturer, and spent 1930–1931 studying abroad at Union Theological Seminary in New York. He then taught at the University of Berlin from 1931 to 1933 and fulfilled the remaining requirements necessary to serve as a Lutheran pastor. He was ordained in November 1931. Interestingly, he was never required to attend a seminary. As Victoria Barnett explains, at this time Lutheran churches were part of "the German Evangelical Church, the Protestant church in Germany. The German Evangelical Church included three distinct traditions: the theologically strict Lutherans, the more liberal Reformed church, and the United Church, which contained both Lutheran and Reformed elements."[6]

Bonhoeffer's academic and personal experiences left him far from satisfied with the churches he knew at the time of his ordination or in the years afterward. By 1931 he had published his dissertation on the nature of the church as community,[7] and in the summer of 1932 he lectured on the nature of the church.[8] The church life he had experienced at home and abroad did not meet the high expectations his writing and teaching described. He became knowledgeable

---

[5] This book assumes some basic knowledge of Bonhoeffer's life. Those who lack this background or wish to trace the specifics of his life should consult Bethge, *DB*; Schlingensiepen, *DB*; and the thoughtful, detailed introductions and editors' afterwords in individual volumes of *DBW*. For an excellent shorter treatment, consult Geffrey B. Kelly and F. Burton Nelson, eds., *A Testament to Freedom: The Essential Writings of Dietrich Bonhoeffer* (San Francisco: HarperCollins, 1990), 3–46. For a very lively and passionate biography, see Eric Metaxas, *Dietrich Bonhoeffer: Pastor, Martyr, Prophet, Spy* (Nashville: Thomas Nelson, 2011).
[6] Victoria Barnett, *For the Soul of the People: Protestant Protest against Hitler* (New York: Oxford University Press, 1992), 5.
[7] See *DBW* 1, *Sanctorum Communio: A Theological Study of the Sociology of the Church*.
[8] For the contents of these lectures taken from student notes, consult *DBW* 11:269–332.

about the lack of understanding between German and European churches and between German and American churches during his time in Spain and the United States. He had become involved in the ecumenical movement and had seen and enjoyed its strengths and been disappointed by its weaknesses.[9] During these years much of the world was gripped by an economic depression. Germany faced extreme unemployment and rampant inflation. Political upheaval was a constant threat. Bonhoeffer felt that the church, the body of Christ, was not adequately addressing the world's great needs through the power of the gospel. Therefore, people could not see Christ because they could not see the church. He wrote in a letter dated October 18, 1931, "Invisibility is ruining us."[10]

His interaction with university students during these two years in Berlin was formative for his future work as a seminary director. He did not simply lecture to his students. He took time to get to know many of them; he took walks and went on retreats with them.[11] Together they began to conceive of a visible community of committed followers of Christ that would seek God's will for their lives and ministries through Bible reading, prayer, common worship, and concerted action.[12] They believed new forms of Christian community building up one another through such practices could aid church renewal. Many of these elements became part of daily life in Bonhoeffer's seminaries, and many of these early students studied with him there.

In January 1933 Hitler came to power. Over the next several months numerous issues plagued the German church. This situation was extremely complex, and no short summary such as the one that follows can do justice to the variables involved.[13] Nonetheless, certain events and participants are important to note. Within Bonhoeffer's German Evangelical Church there emerged a powerful and

---

[9] See ibid., 11:343–89, 477–80; Schlingensiepen, *DB*, 87–93; and Bethge, *DB*, 238–55.
[10] *DBW* 11:55. On this subject, see also *DBW* 5:119–20.
[11] See Schlingensiepen, *DB*, 97–100.
[12] Ibid., 173–76.
[13] For a detailed description of events and significant works on the subject, consult Barnett, *For the Soul of the People*, 1–68.

well-organized movement, the "German Christians." This group advocated a Nazified church that would reject the Old Testament, import laws into the church that forbade Jews from holding office, and generally profess loyalty to the Nazi Party's ideals for a rejuvenated Germany. Jews had already been barred from civil service and education offices by April 1933. The language that excluded them stated that only persons of Aryan descent could serve. Thus, this exclusionary language was known as an "Aryan paragraph."

In early 1933 Hitler desired to unite Germany's twenty-eight regional churches into a single Reich Church, and the church did not reject his wish.[14] An election was scheduled in May 1933 to choose a Reich bishop. Two factions emerged. The German Christians stood behind Ludwig Müller, a loyal Nazi Party member. The other group supported Friedrich von Bodelschwingh, the well-known leader of the Bethel community. Many pastors and churches did not share the German Christians' Nazified theology, but viewed the movement as a splinter group, not as a threat to Christian faith. Bonhoeffer and others thought them heretical and thus a group with which it was impossible to cooperate as fellow believers. Still others thought them just a threat to the church's autonomy and self-governance.[15] Müller lost the election, but von Bodelschwingh soon resigned under extreme pressure that included the government's firing and arrest of several pastors.[16] This resignation meant there needed to be another election. Müller remained the German Christians' candidate.

Two groups in particular opposed the German Christians in the next election, which was held on July 23, 1933. The first was a coalition of younger theologians (Young Reformation Movement), and the second was a circle of pastors and theologians led by Martin Niemöller[17] of Dahlem, a suburb of Berlin. Bethge was affiliated with the Young Reformation Movement. Bonhoeffer had spoken to

---

[14] Ibid., 33.
[15] Ibid., 34.
[16] Ibid.
[17] A decorated veteran of World War I, Niemöller eventually spent 1937–1945 in prison as Hitler's personal prisoner.

the Berlin branch of the organization[18] and had been interviewed by the Gestapo for his part in some campaign leaflets the group distributed.[19] He was also involved with Niemöller's group from its beginning. The German Christians prevailed. The Young Reformation Movement soon dissolved as a protest group. Some members decided not to become involved further in church or national politics. Others, such as Bethge, continued the fight alongside Niemöller and his associates. Many who opposed the German Christians in this election later became the bulwark of the Confessing Church.

In response to the German Christians' victory, Bonhoeffer was asked to be part of a team of theologians charged with penning a confession that set the opposition apart from the German Christians. On August 15, 1933, at Bethel, the group began its work on what would become known as the Bethel Confession.[20] This meeting came at a crucial moment in Bonhoeffer's life. Given the increasingly depressing situation in the universities and churches, he was considering leaving Germany. Bonhoeffer felt out of step with many of his friends since they did not share his belief that Christians needed to separate from German Christians.[21] On July 30 he had preached for and was interviewed by two expatriate German congregations in London. The next day the churches wrote and asked that he be assigned to them.[22] Letters Bonhoeffer wrote from Bethel dated August 15 and August 17 indicate he had decided to accept the London pastorates by the time the conference began.[23]

Two drafts of the confession were crafted between August 15 and August 25.[24] Bonhoeffer abhorred the Nazi Party and the German Christians' anti-Semitism. Unlike some others of the day, he never questioned the dangers associated with these views. He therefore favored the inclusion of a strong statement in the proposed confession of faith defending Jewish people, not just Jewish Chris-

---

[18] See *DBW* 12:24.
[19] See ibid., 12:141–42; 13:30.
[20] For a description of events, see Bethge, *DB*, 300–304; and *DBW* 12:509–13.
[21] Note his explanation to Karl Barth in *DBW* 13:23.
[22] *DBW* 12:150.
[23] See ibid., 12:155–57. Also note Bethge's analysis of events in *DB*, 298–304.
[24] *DBW* 12:510. For a comparison of the two drafts consult *DBW* 12:374–424.

tians. Bonhoeffer thought the document as drafted had acceptable language on this and other matters.

At the end of August the committee chair sent the document to several theologians for critique. They suggested several changes based on their desire to find common ground with the German Christians and avoid schism. To them this seemed a reasonable approach that could preserve the church in uncertain days. Bonhoeffer thought that compromise was out of the question on practical and theological grounds. Writing to his grandmother on August 20, 1933, he observed that the German Christians were under too much pressure to keep any promises they might make. Thus, he added:

> It is becoming increasingly clear to me that what we are going to get is a big, *völkisch* national church that in its essence can no longer be reconciled with Christianity, and that we must make up our minds to take entirely new paths and follow where they lead. The issue is really Germanism or Christianity, and the sooner the conflict comes out in the open, the better. The greatest danger of all would be in trying to conceal this.[25]

The final version appeared in November. Bonhoeffer was so disappointed with the changes that he refused to sign it.[26]

By this time he was already in London, where he served from October 1933 to March 1935. This move did not shield him from further involvement in German church struggles. He was drawn back into the conflict again and again even while in London. Bethge reports several trips Bonhoeffer made back to Germany during these few months. He also notes that Bonhoeffer ran up a huge phone bill calling home for news.[27]

Before his departure, in early September 1933 the German Christians "passed a new church law that included an 'Aryan paragraph,' modeled on the Nazi civil service laws, banning those of

---

[25] *DBW* 12:159. See also Bethge, *DB*, 301–2.
[26] *DBW* 12:511–12. Note Bonhoeffer's statement of his disappointment in the letter to Karl Barth dated October 24, 1933, in *DBW* 13:23.
[27] Bethge, *DB*, 325–28.

Jewish descent from the ranks of the clergy, theological faculties, and religious educators."[28] They also set out to remove opposing pastors.[29] In response to the Aryan paragraph and its exclusionary demands on Jewish Christians (not all Jews) and in support of pastors who had lost their positions,[30] Niemöller and others formed a confederation of pastors, laypersons, and churches called the Pastors' Emergency League. The league had four main goals: commitment to the Bible and the church's historic confessions; resistance to any violation of these; offering of aid to victims of the Aryan clause; and ongoing rejection of the Aryan clause.[31] Bonhoeffer associated with the league from its inception, but he was never its leading figure.

Once again Bonhoeffer wanted quick and decisive action, for he had concluded that the church was in a situation of *status confessionis*. This term "went back to the Reformation and meant that a situation had arisen in the Church that threatened to destroy the integrity of its confession of faith."[32] Writing to Karl Barth on September 9, 1933, he notes that Barth believed that the adoption of the Aryan paragraph meant the German church ceased to be a church.[33] Having stated his agreement with Barth on this point, Bonhoeffer writes,

> Now that which was to be expected has happened, and I therefore ask you in the name of many friends, pastors, and students, please to let us know whether you consider it possible to stay in a church that has ceased to be a Christian church, that is, whether one may continue to exercise within it the office of pastor when that office has become a privilege for Aryans.[34]

As he continues the letter, Bonhoeffer writes the following poignant comment:

---

[28] See de Gruchy, *EB*, 8–9.
[29] See Barnett, *For the Soul of the People*, 34.
[30] See Barnett's discussion in ibid., 35.
[31] Schlingensiepen, *DB*, 137–38.
[32] De Gruchy, *EB*, 9.
[33] *DBW* 12:164.
[34] Ibid., 12:165.

I know there are many who await your opinion, and I also know that most think you will counsel us to wait until we are thrown out. However, some of us have already been thrown out, namely, the Jewish Christians, and the same will soon happen to others, on the pretext of reasons that have nothing to do with the church.[35]

He concludes with a clear statement of his position on the need for a new confession of faith:

What will the consequences be for us when the church is truly no longer one community in every place? What about solidarity among the clergy? When will there be a moment when it is even possible to leave the church? There can be no doubt that a *status confessionis* exists, but what is the most appropriate way today to express what the *confessio* says?—that is not clear to us.[36]

In October Bonhoeffer left Berlin to take charge of his churches in London. For the next several months his main responsibilities were preaching, catechesis, pastoral care, and keeping an eye on the situation in Germany.

Things at home looked more promising to Bonhoeffer in 1934. The Pastors' Emergency League decided that their church was indeed in a *status confessionis*. This situation demanded "a restatement of the faith that would inevitably have to distinguish between the 'true' and 'false' Church."[37] The German Christian position was not one acceptable option among many in the Christian church. Separation was necessary. Pastors and churches that acted on this belief became the Confessing Church.

The Confessing Church set itself apart from the German Christians by taking two clear steps. It announced its commitment to follow Christ alone—not Christ and a government or its leader and ideology—by issuing the Barmen Declaration in May 1934. Though clear on these and other points, the confession did not include a

35 Ibid.
36 Ibid.
37 See de Gruchy, *EB*, 9.

statement of support for non-Christian Jews and other persecuted persons. Then at the Dahlem Synod in October 1934 the Confessing Church refused to accept the oversight of Ludwig Müller, the Reich bishop. For many, including Bonhoeffer, this meant that in effect the Confessing Church now represented the true church in Germany. Victoria Barnett points out the importance of noting that many in the Confessing Church did not reject Hitler or the Nazi Party when they took this step. They treated church matters as separate from political ones. To them these issues were interrelated, but not identical.[38]

By the end of the year, six thousand pastors had joined the Pastors' Emergency League, so there seemed to be firm opposition to the German Christians and their ideology.[39] Bonhoeffer's London congregants added their voice to the opposition by affiliating with the Confessing Church on November 5, 1934.[40] As time passed, stern church and government measures put such financial, legal, and sociological stress on the Confessing Church that opposition became extremely difficult in every way. One could argue that 1934 was the movement's high point.

One result of the events that led to Barmen and Dahlem was that many Confessing Church candidates for ministry could not or did not want to study at established seminaries or serve in state-supported parishes that did not affiliate with the Confessing Church.[41] For example, in October 1934 Bethge was one of fifteen students expelled from the seminary at Wittenberg for supporting the Confessing Church.[42] Also, the Confessing Church could hardly expect seminaries mixing Nazi ideology and Christian faith to provide good ministerial training.

Given this new and constantly developing situation, the Confessing Church decided to provide its students with suitable alternative

---

[38] Barnett makes this point throughout *For the Soul of the People*.
[39] For a succinct description of events, consult Schlingensiepen, *DB*, 114–43.
[40] Bethge, *DB*, 395.
[41] For an example of how these courageous students stood for the faith, see the letter from Berlin seminarians in *DBW* 12:149.
[42] See de Gruchy, *EB*, 12–13.

seminary education by opening new seminaries. This step entailed risk and expense. It provoked a strong response from opponents. Over the next several months the government took structural and financial steps to bring all church factions under its control. Thus, the Confessing Church seminaries were technically illegal from the day they started.

In June 1934 persons involved in planning the seminaries sounded out Bonhoeffer's interest in leading one of them, and by July 1934[43] he was formally invited to do so. He pondered the possibility before accepting. He had reasons to make this move. He had impeccable academic and pastoral credentials. Though not present at Barmen, he embraced the confession as a declaration of the Confessing Church's identity as the true church in Germany. He would feel as strongly about the Dahlem declarations.[44]

He also believed a new type of theological training was needed for pastors. As he thought over the offer, he wrote to Erwin Sutz on September 11, 1934, that he was struggling with his decision. His letter states why he found the opportunity attractive:

> I no longer believe in the university; in fact I never really have believed in it—to your chagrin! The next generation of pastors, these days, ought to be trained entirely in church-monastic schools, where the pure doctrine, the Sermon on the Mount, and worship are taken seriously—which for all three of these things is simply not the case at the university and under the present circumstances is impossible.[45]

He clearly felt the current situation demanded action that would not have been contemplated previously.

Part of his struggle was that the offer came at a time Bonhoeffer was pondering beginning the type of community he and his students had discussed in 1932–1933. He wrote his grandmother on May

---

[43] Bethge, *DB*, 410–11; see also the June 9, 1934, diary entry by Julius Rieger in *DBW* 13:155–56.
[44] Note, for instance, Bonhoeffer's letter to Henry Louis Henriod dated July 12, 1934, in *DBW* 13:179–81; and his support of the document "To Our Brothers in Ministry," dated July 30, 1935, in *DBW* 14:84–86.
[45] *DBW* 13:217.

22, 1934, stating that he wanted to go to India to see firsthand how Gandhi had developed his community because he was thinking about starting such a group himself.[46] Letters dated June 14, 15, and 24 from Hardy and Eberhard Arnold indicate that Bonhoeffer had spoken to Hardy Arnold about beginning a community based on the Sermon on the Mount that shared common financial resources and maintained a rigorous worship program. The letters reveal that Bonhoeffer thought some of the community members ought to be future pastors, and that he preferred all members be single, since he doubted married persons could commit to the community life he envisioned. These letters mention Bonhoeffer's belief that students from Bonn, Berlin, and Tübingen were interested. They also reflect the logistical difficulties associated with getting such a project started.[47]

Despite his concerns and desire to go to India, a few days after sending the letter to Sutz he accepted the position.[48] Perhaps he thought he could best combine his hopes for the church and its ministers through theological training. He certainly incorporated parts of his community vision into the seminary. After accepting this call, Bonhoeffer visited several theological colleges in Britain to gain models, and opened the seminary in April 1935. He entered this work with great enthusiasm, for he believed in it wholeheartedly. The assignment fit him quite well. It allowed him to shape ministerial candidates who could lead church renewal. It also allowed him to continue preaching, writing, engaging in ecumenical and Confessing Church activities, and preparing confirmation candidates.

Bonhoeffer's Students

Every seminary has some method for gathering a student body. Academic qualifications, denominational affiliation, future ministry prospects, and personal suitability for ministry are all considerations, or at least should be. Students today often consider cost,

---

[46] See ibid., 13:151–53.
[47] See ibid., 13:158–63, 164–66.
[48] Bethge, *DB*, 411.

accessibility, faculty members, the seminary's setting, and the seminary's curriculum when seeking a place to continue preparation for ministry. These factors were not irrelevant to those who studied at Bonhoeffer's seminaries, but his students hardly chose the school that gave them the best financial deal or offered them the most security and prestige.

Bonhoeffer's students were, generally speaking, dedicated and adventurous unmarried young men. They chose to align themselves with a new, struggling, and relatively undefined protest church. The Confessing Church included Lutheran and Reformed congregations, so the students came from more than one theological tradition. The Confessing Church accepted the financial obligations associated with its students' attending seminary. Their basic financial needs were met while they were in seminary. When Bonhoeffer welcomed his first students in April 1935, the Barmen Declaration and Dahlem Synod were only months in the past. Most of the arrests and murders the Confessing Church endured lay in the future. As was noted in chapter 1, some students, including Bethge, had been dismissed from a seminary that cooperated with the government.[49] Others had waited for the new seminaries to open. A few had studied with Bonhoeffer in Berlin. All were bold enough to challenge the status quo in German church life.

The students had studied theology at a university and had passed a first ordination examination. They had spent some time as ministry apprentices. For many of them their university studies had been a fairly deadening spiritual experience, according to Bonhoeffer.[50] Regardless, they were not novices in theological thinking. Bonhoeffer was not expected to give them the basics of biblical study, theology, and philosophy. He was expected to build on what they had received in these subjects and to aid them in the thinking and practices needed in pastoral ministry, skills they had not received at university. As was noted above, Bonhoeffer believed that the time was coming when the whole preparation for ministry had to come

---

[49] Ibid., 425.
[50] See *DBW* 14:253.

from communities of faith, not from universities uncommitted to the Bible in general and the teachings of Jesus in particular.[51]

A memo written by Bonhoeffer and the other Confessing Church seminary directors in April 1936 provides some specific qualifications for candidates for pastoral office in the church. First, candidates would be committed persons, individuals who knew that their calling "demands the entire person. It demands a life under the word of God. Every day must stand under the discipline of this word."[52] Second, to place themselves under God's Word, the candidates would foster daily habits of Bible reading, meditation, and holy living.[53] Third, they would pledge themselves to brotherhood with one another and obedience to the church authorities.[54] Fourth, when engaging as a citizen, a candidate would "serve the truth alone and understand himself to be accountable only to the word of God."[55]

Fifth, the seminary directors wanted candidates able to conduct daily Bible reading at a high level:

> The candidate should make it his duty to read a section of the New Testament and the Old Testament daily in the original language. The expectation is that by so doing, he will come to know the entire New Testament and important parts of the Old Testament in the original text and will have worked through several texts with scholarly aids (concordances, dictionaries, commentaries).[56]

Sixth, a candidate was to have "thorough acquaintance with the confessional writings of his church and be completely accountable with regard to them."[57] Since the church had both Lutheran and Reformed congregations, the directors wanted pastoral candidates to be familiar with both confessional traditions. This familiarity

---

[51] See his letter to Erwin Sutz dated September 11, 1934, in *DBW* 13:216–18.
[52] See *DBW* 14:171.
[53] Ibid., 14:172.
[54] Ibid.
[55] Ibid.
[56] Ibid., 14:173.
[57] Ibid.

would then give them the ability to deal with contemporary world-views.[58] Seventh, each candidate was to have spent some time as an apprentice with a fellow pastor who prayed with him and guided his work.[59]

The candidates' time in seminary was viewed as "a final six months of peace and quiet in which to prepare . . . for ministry."[60] The candidates were expected to be full-time at the seminary; the seminary was expected to provide them with fellowship, accountability in daily spiritual disciplines, further biblical studies, pastoral care skills, and preaching opportunities.[61] Finally, "Despite the work load, the seminary period should be a time of quiet reflection with regard to the office for which the candidate should be prepared to assume at ordination."[62]

There were never large numbers of candidates in Bonhoeffer's care. All told, in five years he was able to prepare ten separate groups of students at the various locations he eventually utilized.[63] Estimates vary a bit in books on Bonhoeffer, given the lack of complete records, but the total number of students listed in *Bonhoeffer's Works* is 181, with 113 attending the first five sessions and 68 attending the last five.[64] Bonhoeffer's inaugural group numbered 23.[65]

Bonhoeffer's students did not just suffer inconveniences associated with casting their lot with a fledgling church and seminary. They endured outright persecution from the government during and after their course of study. Bonhoeffer states in a circular letter to former students dated December 20, 1937, that twenty-seven of them had spent some time in prison.[66] Most were denied positions in churches. As a result, they were tempted to cooperate with the government in exchange for parishes with salaries and vicarages.

---

[58] Ibid.
[59] Ibid., 14:174.
[60] Ibid.
[61] Ibid.
[62] Ibid., 14:175.
[63] Schlingensiepen, *DB*, 210–11.
[64] See *DBW* 14:1022–26; 15:592–94. The editors of *DBW* 15 list a total of sixty-eight students in the last five sessions, but they place a question mark beside several names.
[65] Bethge, *DB*, 425. See also *DBW* 14:1050.
[66] *DBW* 15:20.

This was particularly hard for men who had married. Some acquiesced, the first in late 1935.[67] Most were drafted into the army and placed in the heaviest fighting. The first former student died in combat in September 1939 during the initial battles of the Second World War.[68] Many more followed.

It is not easy to summarize such students.[69] Nonetheless, certain things are clear. First, they took theology, ecclesiology, and pastoral work seriously, indeed, as life-and-death matters. They were not simply studying theology out of general interest, and they were not seeking an easy path to a secure career. They were prepared and able to handle difficult academic subject matter. Second, they were willing to pay a high price for their convictions. They were barred from traditional seminaries, and they had no guarantees of employment. Eventually, the Nazi political-military machine crushed many of them. Third, as will be noted below, they accepted living conditions that were less than desirable during seminary days. Fourth, they were willing to study with candidates from other Christian traditions; bedrock confessional issues mattered most. Fifth, they were human. They did not always enjoy the regimen Bonhoeffer put them through. They were tempted by position, prestige, patriotism, and desires for personal normalcy. Bonhoeffer reports that they faced sexual temptations as well.[70] They were not angels masquerading as human beings, and they were not zealots longing for martyrdom. Overall, one cannot fail to be impressed with their dedication and promise.

The Settings of Bonhoeffer's Seminary Ministry

Bonhoeffer welcomed his initial students to fairly spartan conditions. They first reported to Zingst, near the Baltic Sea, to the

---

[67] On this subject, see Bethge, *DB*, 502–3; and Bonhoeffer's description of the student's leaving in a letter to Friedrich Schauer dated January 25, 1936, in *DBW* 14:128–33.

[68] Bonhoeffer relates this fact in a circular letter dated September 20, 1939, in *DBW* 15:273.

[69] Note Bonhoeffer's assessment of three of his students from the second session at Finkenwalde in *DBW* 14:151, 157–58.

[70] See Bonhoeffer's letters of August 2, 1936, and August 8, 1936, to Bethge in *DBW* 14:229–30, 235–37.

grounds of a Bible college. Today we might compare the place to a Christian camp or retreat center. On the positive side, it was close to the beach. Sometimes Bonhoeffer conducted class by the water.[71] This arrangement was temporary, however, so by June 14 the seminary had to move.[72]

The new seminary community settled at Finkenwalde, near Stettin. Though only about half of Bonhoeffer's seminary work occurred there, it is the name most people associate with this era of his life. Finkenwalde "had most recently served as a boarding school and therefore had a gymnasium which could serve as a chapel."[73] Supporters donated basic necessities like furniture and food. Bonhoeffer's own collection provided the bulk of the library.[74] At first all the students slept in one room. In a few months the community turned the buildings and grounds into quite acceptable conditions. A Confessing Church congregation eventually met in the space set aside for the chapel, so there was interaction between the seminarians and local church people. Clearly this arrangement worked well, though Finkenwalde was hardly a plush operation.[75]

But it was as plush as Bonhoeffer's seminarians ever experienced. The Finkenwalde work persisted until September 1937, when the Gestapo closed it down. It was technically an illegal operation from the beginning, but had been tolerated for various reasons. This closing forced the Confessing Church and Bonhoeffer to change tactics. They decided to use the model of "collective pastorates," a system that placed students as apprentice pastors in supportive parishes while they were studying. As Bethge notes, "Similar arrangements already existed among minority church groups such as the West German Reformed Church."[76]

So beginning December 5, 1937, the students lived in two vicarages in two towns: Köslin and Gross Schlönwitz. Seven to ten

---

[71] Bethge, *DB*, 425.
[72] Ibid.
[73] Schlingensiepen, *DB*, 178.
[74] Bethge, *DB*, 427–28.
[75] For a more detailed description of the buildings and how they were utilized, see the circular letter from the seminary to supporters in *DBW* 14:109–13.
[76] Bethge, *DB*, 589.

candidates could live at each location. Bonhoeffer spent a half week in each and alternated weekends, shuttling between two places in a remote area.[77] On the positive side, the seminarians received a warm welcome and determined support from the church superintendents, pastors, and people of the district.[78]

By summer 1939 the vicarage in Gross Schlönwitz was no longer available, so some seminarians moved to the rural estate Sigurdshof (see above), while a group also stayed in Köslin. By the winter term for 1939–1940 there were only eight students, and they all lived in Sigurdshof. Now the comforts of Finkenwalde and even Köslin and Gross Schlönwitz were gone—that is, all the comforts other than the opportunity to study with Bonhoeffer and other like-minded individuals. There was less space, more isolation, no chapel, no church nearby, no real library, less outside support, and hardly any prospect of future ministry for any of them.

After the winter term ended, the Gestapo shut down Sigurdshof on March 15, 1940. There was now no way for Bonhoeffer to proceed in seminary work. His Confessing Church seminary colleagues at other locations fared no better. Their enemies managed to end the Confessing Church seminary work through dogged persistence. Bonhoeffer and the others did not give up easily. They pursued their goals to the end. But they encountered a powerful, determined, and deadly foe.

Daily Life and Work at Bonhoeffer's Seminaries

Owing to Bonhoeffer's writing of *Life Together* and the existence of Bethge's and several others' descriptions,[79] the daily schedules at Finkenwalde, Köslin, Gross Schlönwitz, and Sigurdshof have been well documented. Its aspects will be discussed more fully in chapter 4. The disciplined approach to each day was one of the most controversial aspects of the seminary at the time. It was hard for

---

[77] Schlingensiepen, *DB*, 210.
[78] Bethge, *DB*, 590–91.
[79] See Wolf-Dieter Zimmermann and Ronald Gregor Smith, eds., *I Knew Dietrich Bonhoeffer*, trans. Kathe Gregor Smith (New York: Harper and Row, 1966), 107–61.

the seminarians to accept at first, and rumors of what was happening spread. But the daily routine was based on Bonhoeffer's views of the church, ministry, and personal theological formation. It was not simply a means of keeping discipline, continuing a particular tradition, or pursuing innovations.

Each day, Monday through Saturday, began and ended with approximately an hour-long service consisting of prayers, singing, and Bible readings. There were no sermons except on Saturdays, and the community did not have Sunday services, though, as noted above, a Confessing Church congregation met in the Finkenwalde chapel. The seminary had communion once a month. There were other spiritual exercises as well. For instance, silence was to be kept before the morning service. God's Word was to be the first word heard each day. Bonhoeffer also required thirty minutes of silent meditation after the morning service. During this time the students were to pray the psalms, meditate on a specific passage from the Bible, and offer intercession for others. Many students were amused, baffled, or angered at the imposition. It took a while for Bonhoeffer to work through the matter with them. In time many appreciated silence and meditation, but only after life's pressures showed them their value. Bonhoeffer also emphasized the biblical practice of confessing sins one to another, especially before a communion service. This was not required, but Bonhoeffer set an example for others by offering his confession to a community member. Meals were taken together, and at times books were read aloud, as was common in those days in Anglican and Catholic seminaries and monastic houses.

Of course much of the day was taken up with class work. Bonhoeffer had a great deal to cover as the seminary's main teacher. He taught biblical studies, preaching, pastoral care, catechesis, ecclesiology, and other subjects connected directly to church life.[80] The lectures that electrified the students in 1935–1937 were given in his

---

[80] To examine time schedules and outlines of the contents of classes in the first five sessions, see *DBW* 14:160, 325–842, 1027–36; and for those in the second five sessions, see *DBW* 15:307–85. For an earlier translation of Bonhoeffer's lectures on preaching and analysis of his views on homiletics, consult Dietrich Bonhoeffer, *Worldly Preaching: Lectures on Homiletics*, ed. and trans. Clyde E. Fant (New York: Crossroad, 1991).

New Testament classes and later revised for inclusion in the book most English readers know as *The Cost of Discipleship*. In 1937–1940 Bonhoeffer led students through major concepts in New Testament theology, especially ones related to ecclesiology, endurance in ministry, and pastoral practices. He lectured on confessions of faith, though he never taught systematic theology courses like those taught in the United States. Nor did he offer Old Testament classes the way we think of them now, though Psalms had a special place in his teaching and he taught on selected Old Testament subjects, such as the life of David.[81] Special seminars were held periodically on topics of interest or church concerns. At Finkenwalde Bonhoeffer set aside one evening a week to discuss current topics of mutual interest.[82] Academic work was pursued with vigor.

Bonhoeffer had help with teaching and administrative duties. Wilhelm Rott, who had studied with Karl Barth in Bonn, served as Inspector of Students during the first four terms (1935–1937). Friedrich (Fritz) Onnasch had this role in the fifth and last Finkenwalde term and in Köslin in 1937–1938.[83] Bethge worked as his associate director from 1936 to 1940. These men taught in Bonhoeffer's absence and in their own areas of expertise. Bethge worked particularly hard. In a letter dated June 27, 1936, Bonhoeffer writes that Bethge helped with the confessing churches in Finkenwalde and Stettin. He also carried on correspondence for the seminary with former students, supporters, and pastors. Somehow he also found time to organize a network of supporters, plan visitations to former students, arrange ministry weeks in parishes, teach the students how to lead congregational singing, and help students review New Testament materials.[84]

Rott, Bethge, and Onnasch were also part of one of Bonhoeffer's most famous innovations. After the first session at Finkenwalde, Bonhoeffer decided he needed some men to stay as members of

---

[81] *DBW* 14:870–93.
[82] Bethge, *DB*, 430–33.
[83] See *DBW* 14:1022–26, 1172; 15:592–94.
[84] *DBW* 14:198. Bethge had been called to parish duty, and Bonhoeffer wrote to request his return.

a "Brothers' House" after completing their studies.[85] In the letter requesting the permission of church officials, dated September 6, 1935, he notes that he and several others had "for several years now" discussed "establishing a Protestant House of Brethren in which," he writes "we wish as pastors to lead a communal Christian life."[86] He gives five reasons why this is a practical request: pastors suffer from isolation and would benefit from collaboration in theology and ministry; many pastors now wished to live in concrete communion as a witness to committed Christianity; some Confessing Church pastors needed to be available for emergency situations and for in-depth ministry; parish pastors needed a place for retreats; and the seminary's ministry was important enough to release some pastors from congregational work to help it.[87]

Bonhoeffer then outlines the brothers' tasks. They would provide continuity of teaching and ethos at the seminary, undertake ongoing contact with former students after they entered congregational ministry, aid students at the local university, and help local churches in need.[88] The request was granted. When the second term began, Bonhoeffer, Bethge, Onnasch, Joachim Kanitz, Horst Lekszas, Winfried Maechler, and Albrecht Schönherr constituted the initial group. As some members left, others joined.[89] The Brothers' House lasted until Finkenwalde closed in September 1937. The situation during 1937–1940 did not allow for the arrangement to be replicated.

Though Bonhoeffer's days were extremely full, Bethge notes that he typically left time for recreation and asked his students to do the same. They took walks, played sports, and enjoyed music and singing. Bethge likewise recalls that Bonhoeffer virtually never worked at night.[90] No doubt it helped that he did not have required tests and papers to mark. And he was single. Still, one is struck with

---

[85] See the letter requesting permission to begin the arrangement, in *DBW* 14:95–99.
[86] Ibid., 14:95.
[87] Ibid., 14:95–97.
[88] Ibid., 14:97–99.
[89] Ibid., 14:99. For names of the members in the last three sessions at Finkenwalde, consult ibid., 14:1023–26.
[90] Bethge, *DB*, 429–30.

the balance he attempted to keep in his schedule. As time passed, it became increasingly harder for him to do so. He became quite depleted by early 1939, as will be discussed in chapter 5 below.

One also notices his commitment to spending time with the students outside class. He worshiped daily with them. He ate with them. He recreated with them. In Sigurdshof in 1939–1940 he lived with them and Bethge. When preparing to take a leave of absence in July 1939 he brought the interim director up to date on the students' studies. He then added that the interim director should "take walks or otherwise spend as much time as possible together with the brothers."[91]

Bonhoeffer believed the seminary should also extend hospitality to others. To this end, Bethge describes how Finkenwalde offered sanctuary for people recovering from time in prison or from injuries resulting from mob violence.[92] He also notes that several conferences and retreats occurred there,[93] and that the students conducted missions to area churches.[94] The seminary was not simply a place for isolated study. It existed to serve others in the body of Christ.

Conclusion

The schedule and conditions at Bonhoeffer's seminaries were not unique. Many of their practices of daily worship and devotion he saw also in Anglican seminaries he visited. More recently, Trinity Episcopal School for Ministry had some of these same components when I taught there in 1999–2001. Beeson Divinity School, where I currently teach, includes several aspects found in Bonhoeffer's seminary, such as community worship, community meals, and mentoring groups. The conditions Bonhoeffer and his students endured were sometimes harsh, but not unheard of in protest seminaries. For example, they were no worse than those experienced by students I encountered in 1990 while teaching a short course at a Bible col-

---

[91] *DBW* 15:172.
[92] Bethge, *DB*, 539–42.
[93] Ibid., 433–35.
[94] Ibid., 542–43.

lege in the Soviet Union. The external pressures upon Bonhoeffer and his students were extreme, but so were those that I or friends of mine have witnessed in lands where Christianity is oppressed or Christians persecuted. Like the seminaries just mentioned, the most impressive and most needed component of Bonhoeffer's seminaries is the dedication to sacrificial ministry to others exemplified by these seminaries' faculty, students, and supporters. This dedication is essential to good seminary life and healthy churches. It may not be surpassed, but it should be emulated.

3

Ministers for the Visible Body of Christ

The Seminary and *The Cost of Discipleship*

Discipleship (originally published in English as *The Cost of Discipleship*) would become Finkenwalde's own badge of distinction. For the newcomers the first classes in Zingst came as a breathtaking surprise. They suddenly realized that they were not simply to learn new techniques of preaching and instruction, but were to be initiated into something that would radically change the prerequisites for those activities.

Eberhard Bethge (1989)

Introduction

How Christians think about God determines how they think about everything else. After all, Christians believe God—Father, Son, and Holy Spirit—is the Creator, Provider, and Redeemer of persons and history. He is Lord over all realms of life. His Word defines and directs what is good and right in every person, home, church, and ministry. A proper grasp of and adherence to theology is therefore essential for anyone or any organization desiring reality and God-defined relevance.

It *should* go without saying that theological seminaries ought to be theologically driven. One could be forgiven for assuming that places that receive and send out future ministers would hold and display a robust theology of education. Nonetheless, in a fallen world one cannot expect such to always be the case. Like all human endeavors, seminaries can become infected with unhealthy spirits of the age. They can be battered by financial storms that shatter their nerve. They can face persecution and denominational pressures that divert them from their God-ordained tasks. Therefore, seminaries must take stock from time to time. They must make certain their programs and policies have not gotten detached from stable biblical-theological moorings. That many seminaries drift is a fact. Yet there remains hope that they may come home to port.

Bonhoeffer's theology of theological education can aid seminaries wishing to remain theologically strong, as well as seminaries needing biblical renewal. Living in perilous times, he believed that "everything depended on the renewal of the church and of the ministry," as he wrote in a letter to Elizabeth Zinn, January 27, 1936.[1] In his case, his part in "renewal" included working with others to build a seminary from the ground up. His writings during 1935–1940 reflect a conscious effort to describe seminary life built on Christ, his followers, his body, his ministers, and his wider Christian communities. Bonhoeffer does not cover every conceivable area of seminary work, nor could one expect him to do so, but he does deal with basic critical matters.

The five sessions held at Finkenwalde during 1935–1937 were arguably the theological high point of Bonhoeffer's seminary work. The seminary faced many significant obstacles, as chapters 1 and 2 outlined. Nonetheless, Bonhoeffer had as many students and operated as freely as he ever would. Most of the severe persecutions and temptations he and the students faced came later. Furthermore, the

---

[1] Dietrich Bonhoeffer, *Reflections on the Bible: Human Word and Word of God*, ed. Manfred Weber, trans. M. Eugene Boring (Peabody, MA: Hendrickson, 2006), 10. See also *DBW* 14:134–35.

seminary community included several exceptionally gifted and interested students. A few of these survived the war and had noteworthy pastoral or academic ministries. For example, Gerhard Ebeling, who later taught at Tübingen and Zürich, attended in 1936–1937.[2] Bonhoeffer made time to think and write at a high level.

The most important example of his thought during these critical years was published in 1937 in a volume we know today as *The Cost of Discipleship*. The German title was *Nachfolge*, which basically translates to English as *Following*.[3] While the title *The Cost of Discipleship* conveys the volume's contents in a vivid manner, it may lean too much toward reminding readers of the author's death for marketing purposes. The German title, on the other hand, captures Bonhoeffer's intention: Christian life and ministry require following Jesus, whatever that means at any concrete moment, according to what the Bible teaches. Nonetheless, the English title is so well known that I retain it in the comments that follow. A careful reading of the book demonstrates the importance of pursuing the "following Christ" theme.

Bonhoeffer delivered several portions of this famous volume in his New Testament lectures to students at Finkenwalde.[4] Bethge notes that Bonhoeffer had devised the thesis and conclusions by 1933. He also states that Bonhoeffer added and subtracted many things when forming the book for publication.[5] Still, whole sections of the lectures went directly into the volume.[6] When the volume appeared, Bonhoeffer wrote in a circular letter that the students would know what was in the book.[7] The letter from the Finkenwalde students to supporters dated August 5, 1935, states:

> The course that has probably made the strongest impression on us is Discipleship in the New Testament. Dr. Bonhoeffer presents

---

[2] *DBW* 15:654.
[3] On this point, see *DBW* 4:4; 5:112n5
[4] Bonhoeffer also gave lectures on discipleship at the University of Berlin in the winter term of 1935–1936.
[5] Bethge, *DB*, 450–52, 458.
[6] For an analysis of the part Bonhoeffer's lectures played in the composition of the book, see *DBW* 4:24–28; and Bethge, *DB*, 450–60.
[7] *DBW* 15:21.

an exegesis of the call stories, of Jesus' statements concerning discipleship, and currently also of the Sermon on the Mount. Probably no one is unaffected by the seriousness with which these New Testament findings have drawn our attention to the phenomenon of discipleship. Discipleship is the unconditional, sole commitment to Jesus Christ and thus to the cross, a commitment whose content cannot wholly be articulated. The place to which the church is called is the cross, and the only form in which the church can exist is discipleship.[8]

Since Bonhoeffer had been interested in discipleship and the church for some time, it was natural for him to begin his seminary ministry with lectures on these subjects. But a deeper issue motivated him as well. As one who adhered to the Barmen Declaration,[9] he believed church renewal depended on a new sort of minister for a new type of church. It depended on a group of pastors formed by Christ reforming the church according to the demands of Christian discipleship within a visible body in a hostile environment. As two of his Confessing Church colleagues wrote in a letter dated February 13, 1939:

> Brotherhood is the essential living beginning of "church." Thus we have attempted a church administration through a "council of brethren," in conscious contrast to all church "governments" that conform to the world. (What does it matter if, after centuries of the secularization of the church, this attempt has not yet penetrated and seized the entire "church"?) Thus the knowledge is growing in us that things can only go forward in the individual congregations if there is at least a beginning of a brotherhood around the minister. . . . Thus in clergy circles it has long been felt that a renewal of the ministry can succeed only when the secularized forms of separation from one another in the official church are overcome by a brotherly with-one-another.[10]

---

[8] *DBW* 14:89.
[9] On this connection, see Haddon Willmer, "Costly Discipleship," in *The Cambridge Companion to Dietrich Bonhoeffer*, ed. John W. de Gruchy (Cambridge: Cambridge University Press, 1999), 174.
[10] *DBW* 15:137.

In short, Bonhoeffer determined that church life had to begin again at the beginning. Therefore, it was necessary to train pastors as Jesus trained the apostles. For Bonhoeffer, there was a desperate need for church renewal, and church renewal began with following Christ for the purpose of building a visible body of Christ on earth. These were the fundamental principles he sought to instill in his students from the beginning.

It is worth repeating that a deep crisis in the German church brought Bonhoeffer and his students together. The Confessing Church had not issued the Barmen Declaration or followed the Dahlem Synod's directions lightly. They did not separate from others over some small matter. They believed German Christians eager to follow Hitler had compromised the gospel and thereby the church. Therefore, the future of Christianity in Germany was at stake. This belief made them willing to risk reputation and future prospects for the sake of God's truth found in God's Word. As theologians, Bonhoeffer and his students required biblical reasons for such radical action. Given this situation, Bonhoeffer addressed discipleship and the visible church to ground his students and their future ministries in God's Word.

To explain what this "following" of Christ required, Bonhoeffer wrote thirteen tightly connected chapters divided into two parts. As the *DBW* edition indicates,[11] the first half of the book focused on discipleship, and the second on the church as the visible body of Christ. Though many themes relevant to theological education flow from these sections, I will focus on his comments on costly grace, costly commitment, costly service, and a visible community.

Bonhoeffer's emphasis on costly grace and costly commitment are instructive for today's seminaries because of how they address the type of students and faculty that should learn and teach there. Bonhoeffer states quite clearly that only those called by Jesus and thus called and committed to obedience have any business at a seminary tasked with shaping pastors. Only those who put Christ above

---

[11] See *DBW* 4:29–32.

self, family, possessions, and future prospects are clearly Christians, much less good candidates for ministry or faculty positions. His emphasis on costly service and visible community are instructive because they highlight how pastors should serve and how seminaries should reflect the church's identity as the visible body of Christ, who took on human flesh. In short, Bonhoeffer argues for an incarnational Christ, church, and seminary.

Costly Grace: The Basis of God's Call

Bonhoeffer begins by discussing grace, the ground of God's call. Whatever "following" means, it does not include meriting God's forgiveness by what we do. Thus, grace must be stressed. But this grace must be defined biblically, and the Bible depicts grace as costly. Grace is not cheap in the sense of being "a doctrine, a principle, a system" or "intellectual assent . . . itself sufficient to secure remission of sins" (43).[12] It is not "a cheap covering for sins" for which "no contrition is required, still less any real desire to be delivered from sin" (43). It is not God's saving the sinner and then leaving the sinner as he or she was before (43). It does not "let the Christian live like the rest of the world, let him model himself on the world's standards in every sphere of life, and not presumptuously aspire to live a different life under grace from his old life under sin" (44). Such so-called grace would be cheap because it "is not the kind of forgiveness of sins which frees us from the toils of sin. Cheap grace is the grace we bestow on ourselves" (44). Such grace cannot save, and it cannot create obedience. So it cannot be the basis for Christianity or Christian ministry.

Costly grace, on the other hand, offers forgiveness *and* a changed life. It is precious beyond price, "the treasure hidden in the field; for the sake of it a man will gladly go and sell all he has . . . it is the

---

[12] Unless otherwise noted, all quotations are from Dietrich Bonhoeffer, *The Cost of Discipleship*, trans. R. H. Fuller and Irmgard Booth (London: SCM, 1959; New York: Touchstone, 1995); page references are from the Touchstone edition and are noted parenthetically for brevity. Though this popular English version does not retain the original chapter divisions, I use it because many readers will likely have it.

call of Jesus Christ at which the disciple leaves his nets and follows him" (45). This grace is wonderful. For it leads those it possesses to seek Christ again and again. This "grace is *costly* because it calls us to follow, and it is *grace* because it calls us to follow *Jesus Christ.* It is costly because it costs a man his life, and it is grace because it gives a man the only true life" (45). It is costly because "it cost God the life of his son . . . and what has cost God much cannot be cheap for us" (45).

Costly grace does not provide a set list of rules for Christians to follow. Rather, "Costly grace confronts us as a gracious call to follow Jesus, it comes as a word of forgiveness to the broken spirit and the contrite heart" (45). It requires us to take up the yoke of Christ, but this yoke is easy and Christ's burden light (Matt. 11:25–30). Christ called his disciples to leave all and follow him. The results of this call to costly grace resound throughout the book of Acts. They also resound in the life of Martin Luther, who left the cloister to follow Christ (48–49).

By the time he delivered his lectures in Finkenwalde, Bonhoeffer felt that among German Lutherans grace had become "a principle" (see 43). If one mentally assented to the mere idea of grace in Christ, then one was fine as far as most German Lutherans of the era were concerned (51). Too many people thought that they could not be saved by works, so they would do no works at all (51)! As a result, he argues, "We Lutherans have gathered like eagles around the carcase of cheap grace, and there we have drunk of the poison which has killed the life of following Christ" (53). Bonhoeffer claims that Lutherans had made "grace available on the cheapest and easiest terms" and had left "the following of Christ to legalists, Calvinists, and enthusiasts—and all this for the sake of grace" (53).

Perhaps one could argue that at some points in church history such unbiblical thinking can cause minimal damage. Bonhoeffer and his students did not live in such a time. They lived in times of crisis, when people blurred the lines between the lordship of

Jesus Christ and the leadership of Adolf Hitler. They lived in days, Bonhoeffer believed, when whatever one's views, it was time "to admit that we no longer stand in the path of true discipleship. We confess that, although our Church is orthodox as far as her doctrine of grace is concerned, we are no longer sure that we are members of a Church which follows its Lord" (55). This meant it was essential for Bonhoeffer, his students, the Confessing Church, and all believers to "attempt to recover a true understanding of the mutual relation between grace and discipleship" (55). As far as he was concerned, "it is becoming clearer every day that the most urgent problem besetting our Church is this: How can we live the Christian life in the modern world?" (55).

As serious as costly grace sounds, Bonhoeffer sees it as the key to joy. Humble believers who embrace costly grace are truly happy. They rejoice that their citizenship is in heaven; thus they are "truly free to live their lives in this world" (56). Bonhoeffer observes, "Happy are they who know that discipleship simply means the life which springs from grace, and that grace simply means discipleship. . . . For them the word of grace has proved a fount of mercy" (56).

Bonhoeffer believed his students had to accept costly grace as the basis for their calling as ministers. God saved them by grace that cost God his Son. This concrete grace transcends any abstract principle or any theoretical theological discussion. It originates in and flows from Jesus Christ. It is the foundation for salvation, freedom, and joy. The congregations of the day were not likely to understand this costly grace, Bonhoeffer implies, so these budding ministers had to teach it and live it before them. Bonhoeffer thus informs his students that they are not simply part of a "cutting edge movement" with the German church. They are in the vanguard of a gospel work in a currently ineffective church. Such words must have been hard for the students to accept, and they remain hard to accept today. Yet these words steeled the students for a future difficult beyond their imaginations. Bonhoeffer sensed the hard times ahead, yet even he could not have been fully aware of what would transpire. He was preparing himself, not just his students.

Costly Calling: The Word of Christ

Having examined the situation he and his students faced and the basis for their salvation through Christ alone, Bonhoeffer then proceeds to explain how one hears and obeys the call to follow Christ. He grounds his comments firmly in the Gospels' accounts of Jesus's summoning of his followers. Bonhoeffer clearly views these accounts as paradigmatic for all believers, but especially so for those who would continue the apostles' work as ministers of the gospel of Jesus Christ.

Bonhoeffer begins with the fact that Christ's call comes from him alone. No disciple may call himself (60–61). When the call comes, one must accept it as Christ's word. There is no set program or well-trodden path one may count on when following Christ's call (58). There is only walking the path Jesus chooses. Also, following the call "has not the slightest value in itself, it is quite devoid of significance and unworthy of consideration" (58). Discipleship means following Jesus without regard to human approval. It means acting in concrete ways; it is no mere idea or ideal (59). There is no way to idealize or rationalize following Christ. There is no way to know where the call will take the disciple, and in any case the steps along the way are not up to the one called. So those who place conditions on their acceptance of the call do not understand it. Following Jesus requires action. Matthew had to leave his post as a tax collector. Peter had to leave his family's fishing business. They could not remain as they were and where they were and spiritualize the call (63). Change of heart and change of lifestyle coincide.

Acting on Jesus's call is crucial, Bonhoeffer asserts, for "*only he who believes is obedient, and only he who is obedient believes*" (63). He adds, "It is quite unbiblical to hold the first proposition without the second" (63–64). Good fruit results from good trees, and obedience and faith result from Christ (64). One cannot separate Christ and his gifts. Even those who fail to follow due to wondering if they have sufficient faith "are trifling with the subject" (67). Those who obey realize that following comes from Christ's call and from faith he gives. Those who believe launch out with Jesus, however weakly. Likewise, those who hesitate fail to obey (73). Again, acting is the key. These are vital points, for theological students may be particularly prone to such obedience-stalling reflection. Bonhoeffer has no place for such paralysis. Christ has called, and he and his students must follow. They must be among the obedient; they must be among those who believe.

Christ's call sweeps aside all rival claims. It demands "single-minded obedience" (79). Peter and Matthew grasped this truth, but the rich young ruler did not (Matt. 19:16–30). He let money stand in the way of responding to Jesus's compassionate call to forsake possessions and follow him. Throughout history, Bonhoeffer notes, others have used reason, conscience, responsibility, piety, and biblical interpretation as excuses for not following Christ's call (79). Many think we can be poor or take up the cross "in our hearts" and not have to do so in daily life (79–80). Such attitudes reveal, he argues, that "all along the line we are trying to evade the obligation of single-minded, literal obedience" (81). We thereby trifle with Jesus and invite the world's mockery (81). By eliminating simple obedience on principle, we drift into an unevangelical interpretation of the Bible (83), for an evangelical interpretation requires obeying Jesus's words.

If left to ourselves, however, we will not follow. Following flows from grace. "With man," leaving riches and following Christ is impossible; yet with God, even this is possible (85; see Matt. 19:23–26). Jesus can forge this type of obedience to his call. He must do so, or the disciple is unable to follow.

By the time Bonhoeffer published *Nachfolge* in 1937, he had withstood many temptations to stray from single-minded obedience. Though only slightly older than his students, he had dealt with decisions they had not yet faced. And many more troubling temptations lay ahead. He could not have known what these would be. Still, he knew he could not serve a decaying national church *and* the Confessing Church. He could not remain in good standing at his university for long *and* lead a renegade seminary. He could not prepare ministers *and* adopt the same methods and teachings used in the past. He had to hear and follow Christ on a narrow pathway. In short, Bonhoeffer knew that he had to learn to take up his cross daily and follow Jesus (Luke 9:23), the next subject he addresses in the book.

Bonhoeffer notes that after Jesus called and taught the disciples, he told them they must suffer and die. Peter questioned this need to suffer, and Jesus rebuked him (Mark 8:31–38). Therefore, Bonhoeffer writes, "Just as Christ is Christ only in virtue of his suffering and rejection, so the disciple is a disciple only in so far as he shares his Lord's suffering and rejection and crucifixion" (87). Following Jesus requires "adherence to the person of Jesus, and therefore submission to the law of Christ which is the law of the cross" (87). Once again this type of following may seem overly severe to many, but it is actually the path to freedom and joy (87–88).

Each believer's denial of self, taking up of the cross, and following Jesus will be different. One cannot predict the path of suffering. But make no mistake, "The cross is laid on every Christian" (89). Every Christian must die to the "attachments of this world" and enter into union with Christ, including the communion of the cross (89). This could mean leaving home as the disciples did, or leaving the monastery as Luther did (89). It could also mean returning home to serve, as the cleansed demoniac in Mark 5:19–20 discovered. What ultimately matters is not shirking the cross, and the best way to take up the cross is to plunge into obedience (91–93).

When Christ calls, he accepts no excuses or special pleading. He does not even acknowledge what we consider normal human responsibilities, for he is the Lord of all these. He knows all about them. Whoever comes after him must put serving him above family or self (Luke 14:26). Those who follow Jesus must let the dead bury their dead; they must put their hand to the plow and not look back

(Luke 9:57–62). Bonhoeffer asserts, "By virtue of his incarnation he has come between man and his natural life. There can be no turning back, for Christ bars the way. By calling us he has cut us off from all immediacy with the things of this world" (95). Christ is our Mediator, so he alone decides how to connect us to the world (97). We may only have what the Mediator hands us, and what he gives us is our only reality (97).

There is good news for those who follow; they do not go through life alone and empty-handed. They receive Christian family members and the kingdom of God (Mark 10:28–31). Thus, those who follow Christ can go with him to the cross "filled with fear and amazement at the road he calls them to follow" (101). These people believe, obey, and find joy. They also find fellowship.

Costly Commitment: The Narrow Way of the Sermon on the Mount

Bonhoeffer had an abiding interest in the Sermon on the Mount. This portion of the Bible had a huge impact on his own spiritual growth. His treatment of Matthew 5–7 has sparked a great deal of interest among scholars. For instance, some contrast his views in 1935–1937, especially his pacifism, with his deeds in 1940–1943. Such studies have their rightful place. Yet my concern here is to examine how Bonhoeffer builds on his assertions in the opening chapters of *The Cost of Discipleship* about his own and his students' call to follow Christ by believing and obeying. He clearly considered understanding the Sermon on the Mount the next logical step after understanding the nature of grace and the nature of God's call. Once his students were certain about the nature of salvation and calling, they had to face the nature of the Christian life.

Bonhoeffer simply follows the order of Matthew's Gospel at this point in his book. By Matthew 5:1 the disciples have left their homes and jobs to follow Jesus. They have journeyed to the mountain with him. They have come out from the people so they can help Jesus minister to the people, whom Bonhoeffer vividly describes as "the lost sheep of the house of Israel, the elect people of God, the 'national church'" (105). Jesus sees these followers and knows they have nothing but him, and thus have "everything with and through God" (105). When Jesus opens his mouth and teaches them (Matt. 5:1–2), he is telling them what they must know and do to follow him and thereby rebuild the devastated house of Israel.

The words that follow in Matthew 5:3–12 are extraordinary by any standard of measure. In a breathtaking series of statements Jesus declares the poor, mourning, meek, hungry, and persecuted "blessed." As Bonhoeffer explains, "He calls them blessed not because of their privation, or the renunciation they have made, for these are not blessed in themselves. Only the call and promise, for the sake of which they are ready to suffer poverty and renunciation, can justify the beatitudes" (106). In renouncing all, they find all in Christ. He is the reason they are blessed even when persecution comes (5:11–12). Bonhoeffer surely had his students' future in mind when he wrote, "The curse, the deadly persecution and evil slander confirm the blessed state of the disciples in their fellowship with Jesus. It could not be otherwise, for these meek strangers are bound to provoke the world to insult, violence, and slander" (114). The world will send such people away, but they will send them to the kingdom of heaven, where their Father awaits them (114).

Such blessed persons "are the highest good, the supreme value which the earth possesses, for without them it cannot live" (115). They are the light of the world (Matt. 5:13–16). Such unusual and valuable people cannot be hidden. They do not simply wait for heaven; they live in the world for the sake of world (115–16). As Bonhoeffer argues, "Flight into the invisible is a denial of the call. A community of Jesus which seeks to hide itself has ceased to follow him" (118). Christ's followers are meant to do good works that draw attention to Jesus, not to themselves (119). This emphasis on visibility of witness emerges again and again in Bonhoeffer's writings. For him it is crucial for grasping the personal and community aspects of church and seminary.

Though Jesus calls a new community into being, this community is not cut off from the past. It is especially not severed from Scripture. As Matthew 5:17–20 makes clear, the Law and Prophets will not pass away as long as heaven and earth endure. Because of this connection to God's Word and to Jesus and his call, the new community will exceed the righteousness of the scribes and Pharisees. This is frankly inevitable, for as Jesus deals with the scribes and Pharisees throughout the Gospels, it becomes apparent that he does not think they know God or the Bible. Regardless, Matthew 5:17–20 proves that the new community will not use the law as a wedge between them and Jesus (121). Rather, they share in Christ's righteousness, a righteousness of One who teaches and does what the Law and the Prophets demand (123–24). This new community condemns and draws the wrath of those who want some other righteousness than following Jesus (125) because they do not know the Law and the Prophets.

So this visible righteous community acts the way the Bible teaches them to act because that is the way Jesus calls them to act. According to Matthew 5:21–26, they treat brothers with respect, and they desire peace with them (126–30). Once again the disciple's obedience comes from Christ: "Only he can speak thus to us, who as our Brother has himself become our grace, our atonement, our deliverance from judgment. The humanity of the Son of God grants us the gift of a brother. May the disciples of Jesus think upon this grace aright!" (130).

Jesus's disciples likewise give a visible witness of freedom from lust and self-serving divorce (Matt. 5:27–32), of truthfulness in speech (Matt. 5:33–37), and of unwillingness to take revenge (Matt. 5:38–42; see 131–35). The church, unlike what was typical of Israel in the Old Testament, "has abandoned political and national status, and therefore it must patiently endure aggression. Otherwise evil will be heaped upon evil. Only thus can fellowship be established and maintained" (145). Jesus's visible righteous servant followers cannot meet evil with evil in sexuality, speech, or the use of force.

They must choose "visible participation in the cross," which puts evil to death (145).

All these teachings lead to a grand conclusion in Matthew 5:43–48. Here Jesus requires love for enemies in the pursuit of being perfect as our Father in heaven is perfect. This brand of love sums up the whole Sermon on the Mount (146). This love is not an abstract concept. It is the taking up of the cross of the visible "community of the better righteousness" that "has left the world and society, and counted everything but loss for the cross of Christ" (153). It is extraordinary because of who the community follows.

Because he expounds the Sermon on the Mount in order, Bonhoeffer now takes a very sudden turn. Jesus has been stressing the visible community's calling and separation from the world. One might expect him to tell his disciples next that they can forget the world around them, or to tell them to draw attention to their cause (155–58). Instead, Jesus tells his disciples to take care not to do extraordinary things to impress others (Matt. 6:1–4). Their righteousness must be hidden in the sense that it must "never be done for the sake of making it visible" (158). Believers find their identity "only in Christ and in his brethren" (161). Jesus's disciples give up self-conscious and self-serving work. They are ready to please God and love enemies without wanting human recognition. This hiddenness extends to believers' prayers and acts of devotion and charity (Matt. 6:5–18).

Those who embrace obedience and hiddenness find it possible to seek God's kingdom above all else. They find it necessary and freeing to serve God rather than money (Matt. 6:19–34). A disciple's eye "looks only to his master, never to Christ *and* the law, Christ *and* religion, Christ *and* the world" (173). Thus, disciples do not look to God *and* money. Rather, they look to Christ, and God thereby frees them from anxiety (178–81).

These truths about hiddenness and trust were essential for Bonhoeffer and his students' well-being. Though he benefitted from his family's social and financial status after he entered ministry,

Bonhoeffer clearly gave up pursuing wider acclaim when he began serving the Confessing Church. At the seminaries, he shared his funds, books, and time with others. As events unfolded, the sharing of time in a short life was his greatest sacrifice. His students also gave up the possibility of secure places in the state church to pursue ministry in the Confessing Church. As was mentioned above and will be discussed in more detail below, the state often tempted them with official ministerial status if they would turn from the Confessing Church. Some succumbed, but most did not. The teachings of Matthew 6:19–34 stuck deep and held them fast, even when steadfastness put them and their families in financial jeopardy. Without question, many of Bonhoeffer's students suffered financially much more than he did.

Bonhoeffer's analysis takes a sharp turn when he reaches Matthew 7. He notes that thus far Jesus has taught his disciples the "extraordinary quality of the Christian life" in Matthew 5 and "the single-hearted righteousness of the disciples" in Matthew 6 (183). In both chapters, then, Jesus highlights the "separation of the disciples from all their old ties, and an exclusive adherence to Jesus Christ" (183). Now Jesus addresses the relationship between the disciples and unbelievers.

Disciples are completely dependent on Jesus for their call, consecration, and separation. Therefore, it is no surprise that they are dependent on Christ for their approach to unbelievers. They never encounter unbelievers on their own authority. Jesus sends them. They come as people in fellowship with Jesus (183), as those who bring Christ to others. They do not view nonbelievers as strangers or enemies. Rather, they see them as people to whom Christ comes through them. They meet others by going to them with Jesus. Thus, Bonhoeffer explains, "Disciple and non-disciple can never encounter each other as free men, directly exchanging their views and judging one another by objective criteria. No, the disciple can meet the non-disciple only as a man to whom Jesus comes" (184). This is why disciples must not judge, lest they be judged (Matt.

7:1–2). They are not independent magistrates testing the mettle of human moral good. They are companions with Jesus, who alone has the authority to save and condemn. Christian love sees disciples and nondisciples with the clarity that comes from receiving Christ's love and seeing all sin through the lens of the cross (185).

If disciples "encounter opposition and cannot penetrate the hearts of men" (187) through their witness, what are they to do? According to Matthew 7:7–12 they must pray.

> The only way to reach others is through him in whose hands they are themselves like all other men. . . . The disciples are taught to pray, and so they learn that the only way to reach others is by praying to God. . . . The promise Christ gives to their prayer is the doughtiest weapon in their armoury. (187)

Prayer and fellowship with Jesus provide power for the disciples. They have no power of their own. Their personal judgment of others' sins is meaningless to God. The disciples' prayers are not. No wonder the apostles refused to give up the Word and prayer even for important helping ministry in Acts 6:1–7.

When the disciples share with nonbelievers, what sort of response should they expect? This question was surely important to Bonhoeffer and his students as they launched forth in a new church. In his analysis of Matthew 7:13–23 Bonhoeffer indicates that he had few illusions. Jesus clearly taught that the way was narrow and few would enter the kingdom. Like Jeremiah's friend Baruch, Jesus's disciples must not expect great things for themselves (Jer. 45:1–5). Bonhoeffer observes:

> The disciples are few in number and always will be few. This saying of Jesus forestalls all exaggerated hopes of success. Never let a disciple of Jesus pin his hopes on large numbers. . . . The rest of the world are many, and will always be many. But they are on the road to perdition. The only comfort the disciples have in face of this prospect is the promise of life and eternal fellowship with Jesus. (190)

Besides opposition and the possibility of meager numerical results, Christ's disciples must accept the difficulty of staying on the
narrow road of following Christ. Later Bonhoeffer described the
journey his students were on as a path of joy that included perseverance amid natural confusion.[13] Here he asserts, "The path of
discipleship is narrow, and it is fatally easy to miss one's way and
stray from the path, even after years of discipleship. And it is hard
to find" (190). This is because to "be called to a life of extraordinary quality, to live up to it, and yet be unconscious of it is indeed
a narrow way. To confess and testify to the truth as it is in Jesus,
and at the same time to love the enemies of that truth . . . with the
infinite love of Jesus, is indeed a narrow way" (190).

The path therefore "is unutterably hard, and at every moment we
are in danger of straying from it" (190). Thus, only those who look to
and follow Jesus "step-by-step" keep from going astray. Those who
watch the path instead of Jesus find themselves in trouble (190–91).
As he concludes, "The way which the Son of God trod on earth, and
the way which we too must tread as citizens of two worlds on the
razor edge between this world and the kingdom of heaven, could
hardly be a broad way. The narrow way is bound to be right" (191).

The narrow way is also hard because it requires more than ver-
bal confession. Matthew 7:15–20 teaches that there will be false
prophets and false teachers who will attempt to lead God's flock
from Christ. Bonhoeffer notes that these teachers may be conscious
or unconscious of their falseness (191). Regardless, he describes
such a person's actions in very stark terms: "He is a prophet and a
preacher. He looks like a Christian, he talks and acts like one. But
dark powers are mysteriously at work . . . his words are lies and his
works are full of deceit. He knows only too well how to keep his
secret dark and go ahead with his work" (191).

Why does the false teacher act as he does? "Maybe he hopes his
intellectual ability or his success as a prophet will bring him power
and influence, money and fame. His ambitions are set on the world,

---

[13] In an October 26, 1938, lecture; see *DBW* 15:416–37, and chapter 5 below.

not on Jesus Christ" (191). How does he succeed in his scheme? "Knowing that Christians are credulous people, he conceals his dark purpose beneath the cloak of Christian piety, hoping that his innocuous disguise will avert detection. He knows that Christians are forbidden to judge, and he will remind them of it at the appropriate time" (191). Again, he may not be aware of what he is doing, for Satan "can give him every encouragement and at the same time keep him in the dark about his own motives" (192).

How can the disciples recognize such a person? They will not do so through mistrust and constant heresy hunting (192). Rather, they will recognize good and bad teachers by the fruit they produce (Matt. 7:21–23). Disciples must be patient. Life's events reveal who is true and false. Disciples must develop closer fellowship and loyalty to Jesus so they can stand when the world seeks to separate them from Christ (192). When those times of trial come, it will not be enough simply to mouth a confession of Christ. It is not those who can speak the words "Lord, Lord" who are authentic believers. Rather, those who will bear fruit will be those who do God's will because they know and follow Jesus (vv. 21–23). By bearing fruit in persecution the disciples show themselves ready to face God's final judgment. Bonhoeffer warns, "We can never appeal to our confession or be saved simply on the grounds that we have made it. . . . God will not ask us in that day whether we were good Protestants, but whether we have done his will. We shall be asked the same question as everybody else" (193).

These sobering truths take disciples back to the basis of their call, back to the costly grace that Jesus provides through his death and resurrection. He alone saves, calls, and leads on the path. Faith can look real to the world and yet be false. What is left? Bonhoeffer writes, "There is nothing left for us to cling to, not even our confession or our obedience. There is only his word and call" (195). Thankfully, these are enough. They bring comfort:

> The end of the Sermon on the Mount echoes the beginning.
> The word of the last judgement is foreshadowed in the call to

discipleship. But from beginning to end it is always *his* word and *his* call, his alone. If we follow Christ, cling to his word, and let everything else go, it will see us through the day of judgement. His word is his grace. (195)

Bonhoeffer concludes his discussion of the Sermon on the Mount by presenting the stark difference between those who follow and those who do not. Reflecting briefly on Matthew 7:24–29, he highlights the passage's focus on the person who hears *and* does what Christ teaches. Disciples may not "go away and make of his sayings what they will, picking and choosing from them whatever they find helpful, and testing them to see if they work" (196). Jesus gives his word "on condition that it retains exclusive power over them" (196). The word not followed "is no rock to build a house on" (197). Storms will ruin such a house. Many of Jesus's hearers were astonished at strong teaching (Matt. 7:28–29). But "his disciples were standing at his side" (197). They were the ones from whom Jesus called apostles and whom he sent to share in his work.

Through his discussion of the Sermon on the Mount, Bonhoeffer has shown that costly grace provides the foundation for salvation. Faith that obeys and obedience that believes reveal those who are Christ's disciples. Bonhoeffer has also demonstrated that ministers come from the body of believers at the call of Jesus to serve with other disciples in Christ's work. Lacking these traits, no one—Bonhoeffer's students included—should enter ministry, he rightly claims. If, like false teachers, they currently desire success and fame, then they should not proceed until they become disciples and until they hear Christ's call. Without such foundations, students build their ministerial house on sand.

Costly Ministry: Shepherds for the Scattered Sheep

It is striking in today's typically free-market seminary context that Bonhoeffer only now moves toward describing the work of ministry. Only those who have embraced costly grace—the urgent and difficult call of God—and are committed to obeying Christ's commands are eligible to become Christ's messengers. Bethge reports that for many of Bonhoeffer's students this assertion by their director was "a breathtaking surprise. They suddenly realized that they were not simply to learn new techniques of preaching and instruction, but were to be initiated into something that would radically change the prerequisites for those activities."[14] Once again, this order of steps to ministry may seem overly demanding to some. However, Bonhoeffer simply follows the flow of Matthew's Gospel. Having examined Matthew 4–7, he now moves to Matthew 9:35–10:42.

Matthew 9:35–38 highlights Jesus's motive and method for calling coworkers into God's harvest. Jesus had compassion for the people he taught in the cities and towns of Galilee, for he saw "they were harassed and helpless, like sheep without a shepherd" (v. 36). Jesus knew that the people had official shepherds; they had priests and scribes. But these were not good shepherds "filled by boundless pity and compassion" for the people (202).

Out of this compassion for the masses Jesus relates the situation to his disciples and asks them to pray for workers for the harvest God has in mind. His plan is to send good shepherds to help the people—if necessary, one shepherd and one person at a time. Bonhoeffer writes:

> What they need is good shepherds, good "pastors." "Feed my lambs" was the last charge Jesus gave to Peter. The Good Shepherd protects his sheep against the wolf, and instead of fleeing he gives his life for the sheep. He knows them all by name and loves them. He knows their distress and their weakness . . . and leads them gently, not sternly, to pasture. He leads them on the right way. He seeks the one lost sheep, and brings it back to the fold. (202)

It seems unlikely that a few people with compassion can bring in a great harvest, but that is exactly what Jesus envisions. This is a humble, not a grandiose, plan.

Matthew 10:1–4 then relates Jesus's calling twelve apostles to

---

[14] Bethge, *DB*, 450.

share his work. Bonhoeffer observes that Jesus gives them special power, for they must do battle with Satan (204). He also notes how Jesus knits this diverse group together: "No power in the world could have united these men for a common task, save the call of Jesus. But that call transcended all their previous divisions, and established a new and steadfast fellowship in Jesus" (205). This fellowship was what Bonhoeffer longed to see in believers generally and in ministers particularly.

What work will these called, empowered, and united fellow workers do? Matthew 10:5–6 partly answers this question. Jesus's first task for them is to go to the lost sheep of the house of Israel. Perhaps this is what they wished to do; perhaps not. Regardless, Bonhoeffer asserts:

> They are not left free to choose their own methods or adopt their own conception of their task. Their work is to be Christ-work, and therefore they are absolutely dependent on the will of Jesus. Happy are they whose duty is fixed by such a precept, and who are therefore free from the tyranny of their own ideas and calculations. (206)

They must proclaim Christ's Word to those he commands them to address. They must preach to their fellow Jews not because they love their fellow Jews most, but because Christ has called them to preach to their fellow Jews (207). As the rest of the New Testament indicates, this limited beginning "turned out to be a means of grace for the Gentiles" (207). Following Christ regardless of his seemingly limited methods was and is Jesus's way to get the big job of world evangelization done.

What sort of financial support can these workers expect? Matthew 10:9–10 indicates that they can expect God to provide for them as they go. Their labor alone will lead to this particular fruit. Bonhoeffer asserts:

> To be a messenger of Jesus Christ confers no special privileges, no title to power or renown. This is true, even where the free

messengers of Jesus have turned into a regular ministry in the Church. The rights of a university education and social standing mean nothing to those who have become messengers of Jesus. (208)

Bonhoeffer's words echoed his experience and that of his students. They could have the privileges of a ministerial class, or they could have the call of Jesus, but they could not expect both. The messengers of Jesus must take on the form of Jesus, which is the form of the suffering servant (209; see Isa. 52:13–53:12). Only those who are free enough to accept such poverty can defeat Satan; only such free people "discern the true nature of the service of the messengers of Jesus" (209).

Who will listen to such messengers? Bonhoeffer has already warned that the numbers of people the disciples convince to come to Jesus may well be small. Yet he is not morose about the possibilities. He claims:

> There are still people praying and waiting for God in every place, and those people will give the disciples humble and cheerful welcome in the name of their Lord. They will support their work with their prayers, and indeed they are a little flock already in being, the advance guard of the whole Church of Christ. (210)

Bonhoeffer had met such people among the congregations and pastors of the Confessing Church. Without supporters of this sort the seminary at Finkenwalde could not have opened or survived as it did. He certainly wished for more such believers, but he was grateful for those he knew.

When the disciples have their message rejected in one place, they are to move to another. Rejecting Christ's Word is a great mistake, but it is the hearer's mistake. It is not the messenger's responsibility to repeat the message over and over to people who think they can believe whenever they choose; the Word of Jesus is too urgent for such leisure (211).

What must such messengers endure? Matthew 10:16–25 states plainly that they must be prepared to endure hostility from friends, family, and strangers. Opposition alone does not determine where disciples serve. Christ's messengers receive their orders from him. He alone helps them know when to leave a place or when such leaving amounts to cowardice (214). Indeed, Bonhoeffer writes, "It is not our judgement of the situation which can show us what is wise, but only the truth of the word of God" (215). Once again the messengers are graciously confined to Christ's methods of ministry.

Any other standard of success places the messenger in danger of eventually fearing opponents. Temptations will come for messengers to desert the Lord's call, for they will be blamed for dividing households and nations (215–16). Yet those who endure and look to Christ's imminent return find the confidence that they will be able to finish the work Christ has called them to do. The fact that Christ will do his work through them is as certain as Christ's return (216). This confidence keeps the messengers mindful that "those who have fear of God have ceased to be afraid of men" (218). They have also learned to stop fearing Satan and the way of the cross (219).

What fruit can these messengers expect their ministries to bear? Bonhoeffer notes the encouraging words of Matthew 10:40–42. Those who receive Christ's messengers receive him. Some will believe. Those who believe and help the messengers in their ministry share the messengers' reward from Christ. The messengers can know that their ministry will bear the fruit of bringing others into fellowship with Jesus. The number and social class of those who respond are not their concern. Bonhoeffer concludes, "Thus, the disciples are bidden lastly to think, not about their own way, their own sufferings and their own reward, but of the goal of their labours, which is the salvation of the Church" (221). Because the disciples bring people into this union with Jesus, his work, and his rewards, they bear the fruit of building the body of Christ on earth, which is the subject Bonhoeffer addresses next.

The Visible Body of Christ:
The Church Community in the World

Bonhoeffer's careful analysis of discipleship has led to a searching description of the calling of messengers for the church. One way or the other, Bonhoeffer's goal in his life and writing was always to find and serve the church so he could serve Jesus. In the last major section of the book he links the individual messenger, the many that come to faith through their Christ-called ministry, the gifts they use, and the ministries they perform to Jesus through discussing the church, Christ's visible body on earth.

Bonhoeffer begins with some preliminary observations (225–28). He notes that readers may offer the objection that the disciples could hear Jesus directly. They could see him. They could ask him what they must do. But now Jesus does not speak, appear, or guide. We are simply left to determine—through interpretation of the Bible, getting advice, and examining circumstances—how to live. Thus, it could become easy for us to excuse ourselves from the extreme commitment the Gospels report Jesus demanding. After all, how can we be certain he has spoken when it is up to us to decide?

Bonhoeffer does not accept these objections. He argues that Christ still speaks directly through the words of the Bible: "Jesus Christ is not dead, but alive and speaking to us today through the testimony of the Scriptures" (225). Jesus is present now in the church through Word, sacrament, and fellow believers (225–26). It is simply unbiblical to claim otherwise. The first disciples heard the Word, believed it, and found Jesus true (226). They did not hear the Word, determine its truth by outside standards, and then decide which parts they would follow. Such a process "is a complete misunderstanding of the situation of the disciples, and of our own situation too. The object of Jesus' command is always the same—to evoke wholehearted faith, to make us love God and our neighbour with all our heart and soul. This is the only unequivocal feature in his command" (227).

The same faith-directed Word comes to us today. Indeed,

Bonhoeffer urges, this Word "is even more readily available for us now that he has left the world, because we know that he is glorified, and because the Holy Spirit is with us" (227). It is important to note that hearing Christ's Word is not a matter of stepping into the disciples' shoes or comparing ourselves to biblical or current disciples. Rather it is hearing and obeying now as Christ speaks his Word in his church to his disciples (228).

At this point Bonhoeffer makes a crucial move in his discussion. He links Jesus's statements about the church with those of the apostle Paul. He does so because he believes that the Gospels focus on the life of Jesus and less so on the life of the early church. Bonhoeffer may not take Luke-Acts sufficiently into account in his statements. Nonetheless, he is correct that "Paul has far less to say about the earthly life of our Lord, and far more about the presence of the risen and glorified Christ and his work in us" (229).

Bonhoeffer then claims that Paul uses terms about the church that confirm, not contradict, the Synoptic Gospels (229). He thinks one should not pit Paul against Jesus:

> Our faith rests upon the unity of the scriptural testimony. It is destructive of the unity of the Scriptures to say that the Pauline Christ is more alive for us than the Christ of the Synoptists. Of course such language is commonly regarded as genuine Reformation and historico-critical doctrine, but it is in fact the precise opposite of that, and indeed it is the most perilous kind of enthusiasm. (229)

Bonhoeffer concludes:

> The Christ who is present is the Christ of the whole scripture. He is the incarnate, crucified, risen and glorified Christ and he meets us in his word. The difference between the terminology of the Synoptists and the witness of St. Paul does not involve any break in the unity of the witness of the scriptural testimony. (230)

Baptism is a key connection between the Gospels and Paul for Bonhoeffer. He writes, "Where the Synoptic Gospels speak of

Christ calling men and their following him, St. Paul speaks of *Baptism*" (230). Baptism is God's gift to believers. They receive baptism in an essentially passive manner; they surrender to Jesus and are baptized (231). Baptism creates a breach between the believer and the world, and this breach is complete, for the "baptized Christian has ceased to belong to the world and is no longer its slave. He belongs to Christ alone, and his relationship to the world is mediated through him" (231).

Baptism is "a gift of grace: a man can never accomplish it by himself" (232). Baptism also indicates "*justification from sin*. The sinner must die that he may be delivered from his sin" (232). This death, forgiveness, and justification occur because the "gift of baptism is the Holy Spirit" (233). The Holy Spirit guides, teaches, and enables the believer to walk in God's way (233). Baptism may be passively received, but the Holy Spirit keeps the believer from living a passive life.

Baptism is a visible act of obedience (233). Just as the disciples came out into the open when they followed Jesus publicly, so baptism provides a visible response to Christ's call. Baptized believers have "died to their previous life" (235). In effect, Jesus called his disciples to come and die (Mark 8:34–38), and for Paul to call them to be baptized is another version of the same call. Once called and baptized, the believer cannot go back to the past. As Bonhoeffer comments, "When he joins the Church the Christian steps out of the world, his work and his family, taking his stand visibly in the fellowship of Jesus Christ" (234). This can be a lonely step. Bonhoeffer experienced the pain of family members who did not share his faith, for instance. Yet as Matthew 19:27–30 indicates, the believer "recovers what he has surrendered—brothers, sisters, houses, and fields. Those who have been baptized live in the visible community of Christ" (234). The gift of the cross thereby becomes the gift of new life (235).

Paul calls these new brothers and sisters the body of Christ (1 Cor. 12:1–31; Eph. 4:1–16). What does this mean? Bonhoeffer explains, "It means that although Jesus has died and risen again, the baptized can still live in his bodily presence and enjoy communion with him. So far from impoverishing them his departure brings a new gift" (236). He goes even further, adding, "The disciples enjoyed exactly the same bodily communion as is available for us today, nay rather, our communion with him is richer and more assured than it was for them, for the communion and presence which we have is that of the glorified Lord" (236). This bodily communion is with, in, and through the church, which is Christ's visible body on earth. This is not just a mystical reality; it is a physical one.

This bodily reality stems from the incarnation. Jesus took on flesh, a body like ours. Indeed, in the incarnation, the "Son of God takes to himself the whole human race bodily, that race which in its hatred of God, and in the pride of its flesh had rejected the incorporeal, invisible Word of God. Now this humanity, in all its weakness is, by the mercy of God, taken up in the Body of Jesus in true bodily form" (237). Thus, a natural conclusion of the incarnation is that "to follow him meant cleaving to him bodily" (238).

If Jesus had simply been a teacher or a prophet, he might only have needed "pupils and hearers. But since he is the incarnate Son of God who came in human flesh, he needs a community of followers, who will participate not merely in his teaching, but also in his Body" (238). As much as he treasures preaching, Bonhoeffer writes, "The word of preaching is insufficient to make us members of Christ's Body; the sacraments also have to be added" (239). These are for the sake of the body. Those who have been baptized have been baptized into death, the death of Christ's body. They participate in this death through baptism and the Lord's Supper (239). They thereby commune with him and demonstrate their entering into his sufferings in the body (239). The body of the baptized becomes one with Jesus, and they thus become his body (240). They are "in him" just as he has been "for them" (240–41).

Bonhoeffer asserts that the communion of the saints with Christ and one another makes a profound difference in how we think of the church and all its ministries.

> Since the ascension, Christ's place on earth has been taken by his Body, the Church. The Church is the real presence of Christ. Once we have realized this truth we are well on the way to re-covering an aspect of the Church's being which has been sadly neglected in the past. We should think of the Church not as an institution, but as a *person*, though of course a person in a unique sense. (241)

Believers are new creations (2 Cor. 5:16–19); they put on a new self (Eph. 4:24; Col. 3:9–11) to share in the suffering of Jesus until the resurrection (241–42). Because they are thus in Christ, they also become one with the other believers who are in Christ, for "the fellowship of the baptized becomes a body which is identical with Christ's own body" (242). Those who are in Christ "are verily and bodily in Christ" (241). The incarnation continues in the people who are one with Christ.

Yet this does not mean that the individual believer disappears. Believers do not become invisible as individuals any more than the body as a whole does. Each believer "puts on the new man," the new life, in Christ as one puts on a garment (242). The believer cannot "become a new man as a solitary individual" (242); nor can he, or she, fail to be one of many members in fellowship with others (243). The Holy Spirit gifts the parts and the whole for service in the world (243). One Christian is sufficient to provide the image of God in Christ on earth, but God sees to it that the individual is not alone. Each one has brothers and sisters in Christ who help make up the body of Christ.

Bonhoeffer summarizes his understanding of the body of Christ by linking this New Testament concept to the Old Testament con-cept of the physical, visible temple of God (245). He asserts that the temple Israel looked for was ultimately the temple of Jesus's body (246; see John 2:20–22). God's presence abides in both—in the temple in the Old Testament and in Christ in the New Testament.

Bonhoeffer observes, "Both aspects of the temple are fulfilled only in the Incarnation. Here is the real presence of God in bodily form, as well as the new humanity, for Christ has taken that humanity on himself in his own body" (247). He adds, "From this it follows that the Body of Christ is the place of acceptance, the place of atonement and peace between God and man" (247). Now that Christ has ascended to the right hand of his Father, the body of the believer is the temple of the Holy Spirit (247; see 1 Cor. 6:19). The church is a spiritual temple "built out of living stones (1 Pet. 2:5ff.)," and it is "the living temple of God and of the new humanity" (247). Jesus dwells in, replenishes, and sanctifies this temple as it walks the earth.

And it does walk the earth. Bonhoeffer claims, "The Body of Christ takes up space on the earth. That is a consequence of the Incarnation" (248). Sinful persons have always tried to banish Christ from the earth, yet "despite all this [opposition], the Incarnation does involve a claim to a space of its own on earth. Anything which claims space is visible. Hence the Body of Christ can only be a visible Body, or else it is not a Body at all" (248). This truth has implications for every aspect of Christian work and lies at the heart of all Christian ministries. Bonhoeffer continues:

> A truth, a doctrine, or a religion need no space for themselves. They are disembodied entities. They are heard, learnt, and apprehended, and that is all. But the incarnate Son of God needs not only ears or hearts, but living men who will follow him. That is why he called his disciples into a literal, bodily following, and thus made his fellowship with them a visible reality. (248)

Since Christ's body is visible, his works will be visible.

Bonhoeffer notes that, after Christ's ascension, the church continued in the concrete acts the disciples had previously shared with Jesus. That is, according to Acts 2:42–47 they continued in the teaching, meeting, and eating the disciples had learned from Jesus (249). These were all physical events that gave witness to Jesus's life and work (249). Preaching, the sacraments, and bodily fellowship are parts of a whole; they are not separable events (250–51). All these claim physical space in the church, home, community, and marketplace (252–54). In short, "The fellowship between Jesus and his disciples covered every aspect of their daily life" (254).

This fellowship creates a brotherhood, a family, of believers. Each person becomes "part of the life of the brotherhood" (254). Through baptism the strong and the weak alike become one (254–55). Slave and free likewise become one, as the book of Philemon indicates (256–57). They are visible whenever and wherever they spend time together: "Wherever Christians live together, conversing and dealing with one another, there is the Church, there they are in Christ" (257). There is no power that can come between them and Christ, which means that not even the government has a higher claim on the believer's allegiance than the body of Christ (258–62).

Nonetheless, the Christian remains in the world, though "not because of the good gifts of creation, nor because of his responsibility for the course of the world, but for the sake of the Body of the incarnate Christ and for the sake of the Church" (264). Indeed, the believer must "remain in the world to engage in frontal assault on it" and to "live the life of his secular calling in order to show himself as a stranger in this world all the more. But that is only possible if we are visible members of the Church" (264–65). In this way the body of Christ is as visible in "secular" work as in "sacred," just as Luther argued (265). All Christian community life shows the world that a new day is coming; the kingdom of God is near (268–69).

These statements on the visible body of Christ summarize Bonhoeffer's views on the church in a profound, compact manner. They bring together ideas from his earlier books and lectures on the church. They also demonstrate that he did not conceive of a seminary as a place where abstract doctrines of religion simply get passed along from one mind to another without human interpersonal contact. It is not a place of disembodied communication, as if such a thing could exist where apostolic doctrine truly gets shared (see 248–49). It is a place where communion between believers occurs, where the concrete acts of Christ and the apostles are reenacted daily. To treat a seminary, a congregation, a family, a workplace, or apostolic teaching as a disembodied entity is equally incorrect as far as Bonhoeffer is concerned.

God has redeemed this body for holiness, for he is holy. Once the believers were servants of sin, but now they are to be servants of righteousness (272). In the Old Testament, God delivered Israel from Egypt, made his covenant with them, secured the people through his providence, and established his sanctuary among them (274–75). At the sanctuary he provided atonement for them. In short, he made them a holy community, a community set apart for his service (275; see Ex. 19:5–6; Lev. 11:44). Now God has set apart his holy community in Christ (275).

On what basis can he do so? "The answer is that God justifies himself by appearing as his own advocate in defense of his own righteousness" (273). He puts sin to death through Jesus's death on the cross, thereby reconciling sinners to himself (275; see 2 Cor. 5:19). Through his Word God "looks for faith, the faith that God alone is righteous, and in Jesus has become our righteousness" (275). This faith includes faith in the resurrection, for the "gospel of Christ crucified is always the gospel of him who was not held by death" (276). What is more, through Christ believers die to sin (Rom. 6:11), so "we are dead, we are justified" (277). God completes his work of establishing his sanctuary on earth by creating the body of Christ (277).

This is no temporary work, since "there is also a further gift than these, the gift of final perseverance, or sanctification" (277). God sanctifies those he justifies. Bonhoeffer observes:

> Both gifts have the same source, Jesus Christ and him crucified (1 Cor. 1:2; 6:11), and both have the same content, which is fellowship and communion with him. They are inseparably connected, but for that reason are not identical. Justification is the means whereby we appropriate the saving act of God in

the past, and sanctification the promise of God's activity in the present and future. (277–78)

In short, he adds, "We may perhaps think of justification and sanctification as bearing the same relationship to each other as creation and preservation" (278). Justification enables a believer to leave old sinful ways, and sanctification enables the believer to abide in Christ and grow in maturity (278). Sanctification cannot occur unless one is separated from the world in the sense of being part of the body of Christ, so sanctification is impossible outside the church (279).

Since Bonhoeffer held this view, it is hardly surprising that he warned his students about belonging to so-called churches that were in fact not churches at all. It is also not surprising that he warns his readers against creating their own standards for serving Christ and that he upholds proper church discipline (280–93). After all, the goal is not the preservation of a human institution. The goal is to stand the test when Christ judges all persons according to their works (293; see 2 Cor. 5:10).

Since God judges by works, the Bible "knows nothing about those qualms about good works, by which we only try to excuse ourselves and justify our evil works. The Bible never draws the antithesis between faith and good works so sharply as to maintain that good works undermine faith" (295). In fact, Ephesians 2:9–10 demonstrates that "it is vitally important that we should be trained to do good works. That indeed is the whole purpose of our new creation in Christ" (296). And the Bible asserts that the "believer will be justified, the justified will be sanctified and the sanctified will be saved on the day of judgement" (297). These promises are firm and sure because Jesus alone is the believer's righteousness and sanctification (297; see 1 Cor. 1:30).

Bonhoeffer concludes the book by stressing that believers are the image of God in Christ on earth (298–99). Once more he declares the visible, bodily nature of the church: "An image needs a living object, and a copy can only be formed from a model" (300).

God's Son died on earth to conform a body of faithful ones to his image (301). These persons show this transformation through single-minded obedience to Christ in response to his Word (304). Anything less is simply not a Christian. Anything less is simply not the church.

Summary of *The Cost of Discipleship*

I am not capable of summarizing Bonhoeffer's tour de force adequately. Part of the book's power comes from its wholeness, yet part of its power comes from its rawness, its eagerness to cut to the chase and cut to the bone. Nonetheless, certain points are clear that relate to the subject of theological education. First, the church itself consists of persons saved by costly grace that God has bestowed on them. Second, believers do not call themselves to salvation. They are unable to do so. Only Christ can call them to God and away from their sins. Third, Christ calls people to single-minded obedience and to service he chooses for them. He calls some to be shepherds of the people, and these persons do his work in his place and in his way. Fourth, the people of God and their shepherds are the physical, visible, and holy body of Christ on earth. They cannot be invisible and be a body. Their homes, workplaces, and congregations display the body of Christ in the world, even if only those with eyes of faith can see that such is true. It is also true that their seminaries do the same.

Observations for Incarnational Seminaries Today

If properly understood, Bonhoeffer's views on seminary education as an incarnational activity of the body of Christ are as challenging as any of his other ideas. Given the Bible's teaching and the realities the Confessing Church faced, Bonhoeffer's comments are not legalistic or overly demanding. They are actually compassionate and practical. They remain so today, for the biblical truths he identifies transcend situations and time. They present us with challenging concepts of committed students, committed faculty, and committed shepherds.

Committed Students

Bonhoeffer makes it plain that students should be completely committed to Christ and his calling in their lives. Why is this assertion so radical today? Consider how most seminaries conduct their admissions processes. In many cases we could hardy be farther from Bonhoeffer's point of view. Many if not most seminaries in the United States have virtually open enrollment policies. They take whoever applies, though it must be noted that applicants usually have to pass a background check and have recommendations from a church, a pastor, and/or an academic. After many years on seminary faculties, including six years chairing an admissions committee, I am sad to report how easily most applicants can obtain these recommendations. The seminary in many cases needs to have higher standards than those who recommend students to them. I recall being in a meeting of the Association of Theological Schools, the national seminary accreditation body in North America, when a speaker made a comment about linking curriculum and careful selection of the student body. Many conferees laughed or groaned out loud, and several made comments along the lines of, "We have to take anyone who applies!"

To put it bluntly, in most cases if one has money, recommendations from a church (often in checklist form), and a qualifying degree (or its equivalent), one is admitted. The money part seems to matter most when budgetary constraints are relevant. Evidence of denying self, taking up one's cross, and following Jesus is not sought, though perhaps assumed. Willingness to leave anything, much less everything, is not required in many cases. For example, in 2012–2013 I saw an advertisement for an evangelical seminary that assured prospective students they need not leave home for more than a few days a semester to gain a degree. I also saw an advertisement for another evangelical seminary that listed ten reasons why people should take an online degree from the institution. One reason was that students could take classes in their pajamas. I think it is safe to say that Bonhoeffer would have considered such advertisements examples of institutional cheap grace, if he could countenance them at all. This is not to imply he had no sense of humor; only that he had no sense of humor on this vital subject.

We must give Bonhoeffer's students their due appreciation. They had studied theology in a serious manner and taken an ordination examination before coming to Bonhoeffer's seminary. They had demonstrated the zeal and courage that marks young people committed deeply to a spiritual cause. Most had obviously tried to accept the cost of following Jesus. Many of these original hearers of the lectures that helped make up *The Cost of Discipleship* served jail time for their devotion.[15] They were serious students, the sort every good seminary teacher wishes to teach and send.

We must also give many of our current students due appreciation. Most have not faced the sort of pressure Bonhoeffer's students did, yet some of our students from the United States have left good jobs, faced family pressure not to enter ministry, and moved great distances to attend seminary. Other very serious students have not needed to leave home because they live near a faithful seminary. But international students from (for instance) former Soviet Bloc countries or currently very troubled African and Asian nations have more than an inkling of what Bonhoeffer's students experienced. These good students from home and abroad dedicate themselves to study and to service. They strive to balance thinking and doing, and they desire to transform individual lives and the whole body of Christ. They demonstrate that they are ones Christ has called.

Certainly these good students are not sinless and are not always willing to accept direction without question. But they embrace costly grace and the need to place Christ and his service above all else. They do not find it odd to change careers, move family to another place, and submit themselves to rigorous study and forma-

---

[15] See Bonhoeffer's circular letter to the Finkenwalde seminarians dated December 20, 1937, in *DBW* 15:20–26.

tion. One does not have to lure them into seminary with promises of ease. They are willing to get out of their pajamas to go to class.

Seminaries must strive to have only this sort of good student I have described. This is especially crucial when forming pastors who will serve as shepherds of God's people. This will mean not accepting people simply because they wish to attend. In turn this will mean having goals and budgets that fit the number of good students available. In many cases this will lead to lower costs, not higher ones, for trying to educate too many people can obviously be costlier than educating fewer when resources are tight.

I say that we must strive to have this sort of student because not all seminary students fit this description. Some seminary students are seeking a bit of biblical and theological information, often because in-depth teaching is not offered in their local churches. Others hope to use seminary education as a pathway into an academic career; often they do so because a college instructor was the first Christian they ever heard speak about theology in a serious, compelling way, and they want to emulate that teacher's career path. Others desire to be Christian counselors and need credentials. A few are hoping seminary will help them sort out their very serious life problems. Still others are very unsure they wish to enter ministry and are using seminary as a means of helping them decide. It is not surprising, then, that there is a problem with student retention at many seminaries.

Because of this variety of people wishing to attend, or perhaps to draw them in the first place, many seminaries offer a variety of master's degrees. It is very rare for any of these to require a particular undergraduate major for admission. Some of these master's programs are as short as thirty to thirty-six credits, which without a relevant bachelor's degree is in effect another bachelor's degree major, not a master's degree. Others are ninety credits or more, which is the standard length of a master of divinity, traditionally the basic degree for ministry. Even if every student in the room is a good and diligent person, the diversity of his or her educational aims is more similar to students in an undergraduate general education course than a major course in an undergraduate curriculum, much less a graduate professional degree program. Felt need and interest often lessen the teacher's challenging task, but the issue of meeting the real needs of such a collection of people is never easy. It is no wonder that some teachers would just as soon teach such general classes in hybrid or online settings.

One reason these students and these degree programs exist is that often seminaries and denominations in the United States are (not surprisingly) very American in how they do things. Rather than choosing and forming the best students, they use the typical American wasteful education-for-employment system of stockpiling as many people as possible. They then wait and see which ones make it to churches, make it in the churches, and make it to the end of a lifetime of ministry. There is help along the way, to be sure, but a lot of students and pastors are too much on their own for finding a seminary, funding their education, completing their studies, and securing placement. We seemingly feel we need a surplus to have enough ministers for the churches. Thus, we train them to compete against others.

Meanwhile there are an amazing number of seminary graduates who never serve in churches or some other religious organization, or only serve them for a short time. This trend increases the cost of seminary education. Many of these graduates are very fine people, and many of them serve in the vanguard of much of our congregational evangelism and discipleship efforts. But they went to seminary without a lot of good counsel and without an understanding of the costly nature of ministry. Some quite honestly come to see they do not belong in full-time ministry. I have great sympathy for these good people. They deserve better teaching and better counsel from their churches. Sadly, many stay in ministry.

Yet there is another quite obvious reason programs multiply and enrollment becomes more and more open. Seminaries are facing financial difficulties that are not going away anytime soon.

The typical response to financial challenges is also very American: seminaries try to expand enrollments to gain more cash flow. New programs and new venues are sought to fuel this growth. These programs seem to yield more revenue when they utilize either existing faculty members who are paid per class above their salary or adjunct professors who are paid per course and receive no health or retirement benefits. At first, new income often accrues. But eventually these programs become fixed costs of these venturesome seminaries. Then the "cash crop" yields less each year and becomes another budgetary burden to bear.

Online classes, hybrid classes, and online degrees are the current hoped-for cash crops. They are the darlings of venture educationalists in all levels of education at the moment. The perceived beauty of an online course is that it is a sheer commodity. A seminary sells credits in increments desired by the consumer/student. Better yet, the commodity can at present be sold to a seminary's own students or to students from elsewhere. It can be sold to in-state and out-of-state residents. It can be sold at a premium price because it offers students flexibility. It has the appearance of being cutting edge, in step with the inevitable wave of technology sweeping the globe, and available to busy people and busy pastors who already have churches. It can be offered in real time, but it does not have to be done in this way. It can also be offered at about the same level as an old correspondence course delivered through the US Postal Service. Most seminaries will be tempted to take this latter route, since the most attractive versions of online courses are expensive to devise and maintain.

Best of all for those to whom the cost of delivery matters most, personnel costs can be fixed at a per-course level. For instance, a man I know came to my office recently. We had spoken before about his involvement in online teaching. Now he told me he taught fifteen to eighteen courses with about twenty students in each course per year. For his labor his employer paid him three thousand dollars per course, but no health, retirement, or other benefits. He now had health costs he could not cover. Using a conservative estimate, his courses generated around ten times the revenue he received. He had no job security whatsoever and no way to know how many courses he would teach the next year. No one made him accept this lifestyle; he is a free moral agent. Yet it takes little imagination to guess what the prophet Amos would say about such practices performed by an institution professing to be Christian.

There is one simple *fiscal* reason to doubt that these courses will save the seminary budget: no such program has done so in the past. Furthermore, when given the same budgetary scrutiny as on-campus programs, they do not pay as well as it first seems. They seem to pay well only if a seminary has full-time students taking full-time courses to serve as the bulwark of the seminary's budget. They work when on-campus admissions, administrative, and computer technology help exists. In short they depend on some permanent structures.

There is one simple *theological* reason to doubt these courses will save the seminary budget, or that it will matter much if they do: they bear no resemblance to the commitment Christ asks of persons he calls to ministry. Programs marketed as easy to take and easy to gain do not sound much like what Bonhoeffer describes Jesus as teaching in the Sermon on the Mount. Programs that treat students as consumers instead of obedient servant followers of Christ hardly fit what Matthew 9:35–10:42 depicts. Where personal shaping of disciples diminishes or disappears, so does Christ's way of shaping shepherds.

It is time for seminaries to focus their energies on becoming more biblical in their mission as they endeavor to be more financially responsible and viable. It is time to focus energy and resources on students committed to serving long-term in churches, mission fields, and other biblically based ministries. Thus, it is time to let go of programs that do not support this goal and of students who are unsure they want to go into ministry. Over time this decision will make seminaries fit the shape of the churches' needs and the seminaries' budgets.

Committed Teachers

It is also important to note that Bonhoeffer's statements about costly grace, costly calling, and costly service apply to seminary teachers. Though only twenty-nine years old in 1935, Bonhoeffer had been privileged to have several formative experiences relevant for a seminary teacher. He had earned an advanced degree. He had written books and articles. He had spent an academic year in the United States. He had served churches in Barcelona and London, and had been deeply involved in ecumenical work. A well-rounded person, he enjoyed sports, literature, conversation, and music.

More importantly, he had developed a close and growing relationship with Jesus that guided his views of theological education and its role in the church. Such was not always the case. It was probably not until after he returned from the United States and began his teaching that a great change occurred.[16] He confessed in a letter written in 1936 that he began his academic career with very selfish motives. He describes his transformation as follows:

> I came to the Bible for the first time. It is terribly difficult for me to say that. I had already preached several times, had seen a lot of the church, had given speeches about it and written about it—but I had still not become a Christian, I was very much an untamed child, my own master. I know, at that time I had turned this whole business about Jesus Christ into an advantage for myself, a kind of crazy vanity. I pray God it will never be so again.[17]

Even before the Hitler regime began in 1933, Bonhoeffer began to grasp that "the life of a servant of Jesus Christ must belong to the church, and gradually it became clearer how far this has to go."[18] By 1935 his commitment to Christ took him to Finkenwalde and led to deep reflection on following Jesus. He clearly asked nothing of his students he did not demand of himself. And he demanded

---

[16] See Bethge, *DB*, 202–3.

[17] Bonhoeffer made these comments in a letter to Elizabeth Zinn dated January 27, 1936. See Bonhoeffer, *Reflections on the Bible*, 9; and *DBW* 14:134–35.

[18] Bonhoeffer, *Reflections on the Bible*, 10.

nothing of the students or himself that he did not believe he found in the Bible.

Not every faculty member can match Bonhoeffer's spiritual and theological depth. That is not the point of my comparison. My point is that we need faculty members who know Christ, have steeped themselves in the Bible and theology, have decided that serving Christ takes precedence over academic position and prestige, have served congregations in some substantial way, and are willing to give themselves personally to students. These are essentials, not optional features. These qualities must be verified, for they mirror the traits for ministers found in 1–2 Timothy and Titus.

This means that, among other things, a seminary teacher must reject the careerist mind-set that afflicts many today. The sort of teacher needed does not speed through degree programs with the goal of gaining credentials and then send off their resumes to whatever sort of place will hire them. They do not "market" and "brand" themselves. They do not view seminary teaching as a way to enhance their scholarly reputations, though that may occur. They do not leave congregational work to what they consider weaker minds. They do not write books because they want to become famous, though that may occur. They do not treat students as necessary nuisances, and time with students as interruptions of their real work, research. Instead they will walk the narrow way of dying to self to build up God's people. Respect and even fame may result. If so, these may well be crosses the teacher may need to learn to carry in joyful service of Christ. Regardless, these must never be the teacher's goal.

Yet following this call also means rejecting the activist mind-set found many places. Some seminaries pay little and/or push teachers into so much church, denominational, administrative, and instructional work that the teacher has no time to think, much less time to grow deeper in Christ, deliver fresh material, or write books that will enrich others. Despite all he was doing, Bonhoeffer considered it essential to give some Confessing Church students the freedom to pursue academic research.[19] He studied and wrote in the margins of busy academic terms and during breaks. Yet he also found time to rest, though he needed to do so more often than he did.

We need committed and balanced faculty and students who know Christ and one another. Gifts will vary. So will the crosses each bears. But faculty and students are the most precious assets a seminary has. If we choose them poorly by selecting them in an unbiblical fashion, our work will flounder or fail. We must return to the Bible for our view of students and faculty, lest in treating them as commodities we find ourselves in a famine of the Word of God (see Amos 8:11–12).

Committed Shepherds

Reading *The Cost of Discipleship* with its historical context in mind is sobering for many reasons. Not the least of these is the type of minister Bonhoeffer hoped to form. The next chapter will discuss this subject further, but some points are evident now. Bonhoeffer desired to send out pastors committed to God's Word, to send out people who listened to God and trusted him. He wanted pastors who had developed disciplines necessary for the hard work of ministry. Daily Bible reading, prayer, praise, confession, and meditation were staples of this minister's spiritual diet, as was love for community. Proclamation, spiritual guidance, and outreach were to be embraced with obedient joy.

All this sounds fairly typical, and so it should be. But one other factor deserves mention. Bonhoeffer prepared persons for a critical situation. He knew the Confessing Church faced overwhelming odds in a time of deep evil. I think he also sensed that Christians in Germany had to face the possibility that churches would be shuttered or co-opted in the days ahead. His statements about "religionless Christianity" later in life give evidence of this dawning realization that all the trappings of religion, such as power, prestige,

---

[19] See Bethge, *DB*, 566–67.

and position, would disappear.[20] It was possible that Christians would not be allowed to meet if they did not please the state. Believers would have to make do with Christ and his people alone.

One could simply write off the sterner statements about the minister's role as special for Bonhoeffer's time except for three very important facts. First, Bonhoeffer's biblical exegesis is sound. His comments fit the Bible's overall conception of servants of Jesus Christ who serve the church in roles of responsibility for others. Second, because his exegesis is biblically sound, Bonhoeffer's conclusions remind us that Christians always live in critical situations, or at least may be doing so at any moment. We can be lulled into thinking otherwise, but such is the case. The world as we know it is not hospitable to real Christian belief. Third, many Christian ministers around the world are facing severe persecution at this moment. We need ministers who can shape a community ready to stand in all sorts of conditions.

Incarnational Seminaries of the Visible Body of Christ

Bonhoeffer refused to let the church be treated as an abstract concept. He did not accept any view of the church that allowed it to be invisible or inactive. To him the church will always be the body of Christ on earth until Jesus comes again. As such the church is the visible bodily form of Jesus, who took on human form to minister to human beings (see John 1:1–18; Phil. 2:5–11). It is visible wherever Christians live alone, with others, or in families, and wherever they meet in congregations or do any other individual or shared work. Christ's body is incarnational and relational by definition, according to Bonhoeffer. This understanding of the body of Christ extends to that body's work in Christian education, especially

---

[20] Note his distaste for hollow religion, expressed in his diary entry dated July 18, 1939, after attending a service at Riverside Church in New York City. He writes that he found "the whole thing a discreet, opulent, self-satisfied celebration of religion. With such an idolization of religion, the flesh, which was accustomed to being held in check by the word of God, revives. Such preaching renders people libertine, egoistic, indifferent. Do the people really not know that one can do as well or better without 'religion'—if only it weren't for God himself and his word? Perhaps the Anglo-Saxons really are more religious than we, but they are not more Christian, if they tolerate such sermons." *DBW* 15:224.

Christian education that forms the next generation of shepherds for God's people.

It would be strange, then, to make a practice of shaping pastors in an impersonal way through classes and degrees cut off from other Christians, unless the greatest crisis prevented personal approaches. To be sure, Christians have long sent materials and broadcasted into areas where no visible Christian witness has existed, or where it would be extremely dangerous for local believers to meet for theological training. However, we have always known that when we are reduced to sending materials to people we do not know, the level of interaction has shifted from communion to communication, or even to mere transfer of information. Historically we have longed for the chance for the Christian people in such isolated areas to know one another and for us to know them. As Bonhoeffer stated, God sent witnesses, not a recording.[21] Christ has a body on earth, not simply a voice in a machine. Even the Bible, God's written Word, is intended for explanation, since God calls preachers and teachers to declare it. It seems strange to me to institutionalize a method of sending out information in a crisis situation when the people and resources exist to do personal education instead.

The visible church should not give up visible seminaries if the church thinks seminaries are a viable authentic work of the church. It may be that new forms of personal seminaries are needed. It may be that costs must be brought into line with resources. I am not suggesting that supporters of seminaries should simply pay whatever budgetary amounts current seminaries request. Yet it may also be that churches and individuals will need to support seminaries at a higher level of financial commitment. My aim is not to defend the common seminary an individual reader may know. My aim is to argue that the goal of the personal, visible seminary is a staple of pastoral formation worth keeping. It is biblical, useful, and proven. It is particularly needed when secular and historically Christian universities and churches do not value the Bible, the creeds, and the

---

[21] *DBW* 15:571.

teachings of Jesus. It is likewise needed when there are a solid number of good universities ready to cooperate with faithful churches. The true church is not invisible, nor can it be. A true seminary therefore cannot be invisible either.

Conclusion

Bonhoeffer's *The Cost of Discipleship* offers seminaries a theology of the seminary's mission, the seminary's recruitment of faculty, the seminary's recruitment of students, and the seminary's goals for its graduates. This theology anchors the ministry of preparing pastors in the nature of the church as Christ's visible body on earth. It is taken from the New Testament, and because of this it can stand the test of time and meet changing circumstances. A seminary that follows this theology will have something lasting to offer its faculty, students, supporters, and churches. It will not necessarily follow all the practices Bonhoeffer adopted. Nonetheless, it will transcend the trends and fads that will likely continue to darken the horizon of serious theological and ministerial study, reflection, and formation.

4

A Visible Community
of the Body of Christ

The Seminary and *Life Together*

Anything that claims space is visible. Hence the Body
of Christ can only be a visible Body, or else it is not a
Body at all.

Dietrich Bonhoeffer (1937)

Introduction

Embracing the theology of *The Cost of Discipleship* includes seeking to create concrete expressions of the body of Christ. For Bonhoeffer this meant creating a pattern of life in his seminaries that reflected this theology. Describing such a community is the aim of Bonhoeffer's next book, *Life Together*, which was written in 1938 and published in 1939. *Life Together* was Bonhoeffer's best-selling book during his lifetime, going through four printings in its first year alone.[1] It has remained popular since.

Like *The Cost of Discipleship*, the book has often been read without important parts of its original context in mind, in part due to the

---

[1] *DBW* 5:21.

forms in which it was first published. For instance, John W. Dober-stein's introduction to the first American edition states that Bonhoeffer was called back to Germany "to take charge of an 'illegal,' clandestine seminary for the training of young pastors in Pomerania."[2] This description is fine as far as it goes, but "clandestine" sounds more secret than the seminary actually was. He then notes:

> In 1935 he moved to Zingst and from there to Finkenwalde near Stettin, where he shared a common life in emergency-built houses with twenty-five vicars. This was life together, the life of the Christian community which is described and documented with Biblical insights . . . here presented in translation.[3]

This description does not represent the building and grounds at Finkenwalde very accurately and implies that Bonhoeffer only had Finkenwalde in mind when he wrote the book, though he had continued the work in other places for a year. The dust jacket of this first American edition states that the book "is primarily a consideration of the meaning of Christian community" in families and Christian groups, which leaves the seminary context behind. Bonhoeffer most likely wished to aid other Christian communities, but the seminary setting was the book's primary focus.

Of course, one must be grateful for these early editions, and readers can gain much from reading the book with a more general purpose in mind. Bonhoeffer certainly supported the forming of Christian communities beyond seminary settings, as was noted above in chapter 2. Yet most of Bonhoeffer's specific observations in the book are drawn from his experiences as a seminary director. Thus, for the purposes of understanding Bonhoeffer's life and his views on ministerial formation in visible seminaries, I will chart the basic background of when, why, and how he wrote the book. I will then discuss the book's five chapters and their importance for understanding Bonhoeffer's view that a seminary, like other

---

[2] See Dietrich Bonhoeffer, *Life Together*, trans. John W. Doberstein (New York: Harper and Row, 1954), 10.
[3] Ibid., 10–11.

communities of faith, is a visible community of the body of Christ. I will then draw some conclusions for seminaries practicing life together today.

The Writing of *Life Together*

As was outlined above, Bonhoeffer led five seminary sessions at Zingst (April 26 to June 14, 1935) and Finkenwalde (June 24, 1935, to September 8, 1937).[4] Bethge writes that as the fifth course was ending, Bonhoeffer completed "his *Discipleship* manuscript as planned, spent a few sunny days on the Baltic with the fifth student group, and then, on 8 September 1937, concluded the term with the customary farewell party."[5] Bethge adds that Bonhoeffer did not know that a government decree ordering the dissolving of all Confessing Church seminaries had been issued on August 29. Thus, Bonhoeffer was surprised to learn on September 28, 1937, that the Gestapo had sealed Finkenwalde. The other Confessing Church seminaries soon met the same fate.[6] Finkenwalde's closing meant Bonhoeffer had lost his home, not just his seminary. The Brothers' House also ceased, which was a blow to his view of how the seminary could best serve the church and the students. He would now have to carry on without as many brothers to share the work and share his life. The difficulty of following Christ as Bonhoeffer had described in *The Cost of Discipleship* once again became quite evident.

By December 5, 1937, the seminary work continued in two locations.[7] Though the Brothers' House could not continue, Bonhoeffer, Bethge, and Onnasch, who had all been part of it,[8] led the work. Bonhoeffer now had to shuttle between two sites, so he could not share life with all the seminarians the way he had in Zingst and Finkenwalde. Nonetheless, he had ensured that the students had

---

[4] See *DBW* 14:1015–36; and Bethge, *DB*, 1026.
[5] Bethge, *DB*, 584.
[6] Ibid.
[7] See the descriptions of the sites in chapter 2.
[8] See the list of members in *DBW* 14:1023–26.

like-minded colleagues of his in both places. Daily worship and meditation continued. But given the closing of Finkenwalde and the increasingly difficult political situation, Bonhoeffer did not know how long the seminary work could go on in its current form.

Between December 5, 1937, and September 9, 1938, two more sessions were completed. Approximately thirty-one more students had received training.[9] Meanwhile, momentous personal, world, and church events transpired.[10] Bonhoeffer was banned from residing in Berlin in January 1938, though he was subsequently given permission to visit his parents' home, which he did often. Germany occupied Austria in March. In June, Bonhoeffer led a conference for forty-five of his former seminarians. At this gathering he gave lectures on temptation aimed in large part at helping the young theologians resist seeking legalized status with the government. At the sixth Confessing Church synod, held in July, the church gave pastors permission to take an oath of loyalty to Hitler. In September Germany began the process that led to the occupation of Czecho-slovakia. With the possibility that the Czechoslovakian situation would bring on war, Bonhoeffer helped his brother-in-law (who was of Jewish descent) and his twin sister, Sabine, move from Göttingen that month. They soon settled in England. Bethge and Bonhoeffer stayed in the family home in Göttingen for four weeks to have a bit of a respite from all their activity and to guard the home.

Though it is a wonder he could think clearly at all, Bonhoeffer wrote the basic manuscript of *Life Together* in those four weeks. With uncertainty all around him, he wished to commit to writing the principles and practices he had put in place at Finkenwalde and was continuing in Gross Schlönwitz and Köslin. He also desired to note how other types of Christian communities (such as he envisioned when thinking about going to India in 1934) might use these ideas, for in the book's preface he writes, "The variety of new ecclesial forms of community makes it necessary to enlist

---

[9] *DBW* 15:585–87, 592–93.
[10] The list of events that follows comes from *DBW* 15:586–87.

the vigilant cooperation of every responsible party."[11] Even more so than *The Cost of Discipleship*, there is an unvarnished, urgent tone in the prose that is part of the book's beauty. Under these time constraints Bonhoeffer wrote concisely, and with great hope and wisdom.

The Visible Christian Community

The book unfolds in five relatively brief and clearly argued chapters. Each chapter builds on Bonhoeffer's statements about the visible body of Christ found in *The Cost of Discipleship* and several of his other previous writings. Each treats the community as the body of Christ living, worshiping, learning, and serving together. As he stated in his letter requesting permission to begin the Brothers' House, he believed that seminary was a time for students to learn how to lead a faithful Christian community. They could best do this by participating in such a community first. What he describes is a minimum experience for them that he did not deem optional. His account of what he intended at his seminaries begins with an introduction to the concept of community and proceeds in his successive chapters to detail four particular aspects of that community.

Community as Gift and Challenge

Bonhoeffer begins by noting that life together under God's Word is a wonderful gift (27). Indeed, he writes, "The Christian cannot simply take for granted the privilege of living among other Christians. Jesus Christ lived in the midst of his enemies. In the end all his disciples abandoned him. On the cross he was all alone" (27). Christians also live among enemies. They do so for the same reason Jesus did, which was to bring these enemies to God (27). Since the church is Christ's body, things could be no other way. The Bible was sufficient evidence for Bonhoeffer's point about living among

---

[11] *DBW* 5:25. All subsequent quotations from *Life Together* are from *DBW* 5, and page numbers are noted parenthetically instead of footnoted.

enemies, but he had of course also experienced severe opposition to Christ and his people by now.

Christ's enemies often succeed in isolating believers through persecution and imprisonment. Furthermore, normal life brings isolation through illness, old age, or missionary service (28). Since so many Christians do not have regular community, those who have such community know that it "is by God's grace that a congregation is permitted to gather visibly around God's word and sacrament in this world" (28). Those who cannot meet with fellow believers "know that visible community is grace" (28). Happily, the Bible promises that in the new heavens and earth the body of Christ will be together forever with Christ (28). All lonely persons can therefore look to the Scriptures for hope and comfort in times of desolation caused by lack of community fellowship (28). These reflections are particularly meaningful as one recalls that Bonhoeffer wrote them in his twin sister's former home after she and her family were forced to leave Germany.

Bonhoeffer next notes that the desire for face-to-face fellowship is typical of biblical writers.[12] Paul longed to see the Thessalonians (1 Thess. 3:10), and as he awaited death he wished to see Timothy (2 Tim. 1:4). The apostle John wrote epistles stating that he could have written more but desired to speak with the recipients face-to-face (29; see 2 John 12; 3 John 13). One could add that Old Testament characters often describe their longing to see God's face.[13] Therefore, Bonhoeffer writes, "The believer need not feel any shame when yearning for the physical presence of other Christians, as if one were still living too much in the flesh" (29). After all, he argues, "The prisoner, the sick person, the Christian living in the diaspora recognizes in the nearness of a fellow Christian a physical sign of the gracious presence of the triune God" (29).

Those who have the regular gift of the presence of other Christians can easily take this privilege for granted, but such should

---

[12] See chapter 6 below for a further discussion of these passages.
[13] I owe this insight to James Montgomery Boice, *Come to the Waters: Daily Bible Devotions for Spiritual Refreshment*, comp. D. Marion Clark (Grand Rapids: Baker, 2012), devotion for March 20.

not be the case (29–30). Given the promises and admonitions in the Bible and the sacrifices made by isolated believers, Bonhoeffer asserts:

> Therefore, let those who until now have had the privilege of living a Christian life together with other Christians praise God's grace from the bottom of their hearts. Let them thank God on their knees and realize: it is grace, nothing but grace, that we are still permitted to live in the community of Christians today. (30)

Letters, brief visits from others, and church worship services are all tokens of this grace (30). So are seminaries: "Before their ordination young seminarians receive the gift of a common life with their brothers for a certain length of time" (30). So seminary communities are a reminder of the promise that believers will be together forever. Bonhoeffer considered them precious communities of the visible body of Christ, places that showed students the way community life in churches can be shaped.

As usual, Bonhoeffer grounds his comments in christology. The presence of other believers keeps one from being alone in the company of enemies, but it is more than that. "Christian community means community through Jesus Christ and in Jesus Christ. . . . We belong to one another only through and in Jesus Christ" (31). Christians no longer live by their own resources. They live through the resources Christ gives them. These resources include salvation from outside themselves. God justifies them through Christ's "alien righteousness" (31). These resources include God's Word. Community members are dependent on God's Word alone for assurance of salvation and guidance in life (31–32). True believers long for God's sustaining Word day by day, knowing that, "In themselves they are destitute and dead. Help must come from the outside; and it has come and comes daily and anew in the Word of Jesus Christ, bringing us redemption, righteousness, innocence, and blessedness" (32).

These resources also include what members receive from others. God has chosen not to give his help without human agents. Rather, "God put this Word into the mouth of human beings so that it might be passed on to others" (32). Thankfully, "When people are deeply affected by the Word, they tell it to other people. God has willed that we should seek and find God's living Word in the testimony of other Christians, in the mouths of human beings" (32). This means "Christians need other Christians who speak God's word to them" (32). To share the good news of justification and God's guidance for human beings, God has granted the gift of community. So Bonhoeffer's view of the Christian community is anchored in the Reformation principles of salvation through faith alone and the authority of the Bible alone (32).

Not only do Christians come together because of Jesus Christ; he alone gives them unity and peace with one another (32–33). Without him they would not recognize one another, and their egos would keep them from loving one another (33). But through Christ "Christians can live with each other in peace; they can love and serve one another; they can become one" (33). For Jesus is their Mediator now and forever (33).

Furthermore, Christ's incarnation means that he took on human flesh forever. Bonhoeffer argues, "This was the eternal decree of the triune God. Now we are in him. Wherever he is, he bears our flesh, he bears us" (33). Not only that, "And where he is, there we are too—in the incarnation, on the cross, and in his resurrection. We belong to him because we are in him. That is why the Scriptures call us the body of Christ" (33). Believers are thereby one in him and with one another throughout eternity. As Bonhoeffer summarizes, "Christian community means community through and in Jesus Christ. Everything the Scriptures provide in the way of directions and rules for Christians' life together rests on this presupposition" (33).

The Bible describes this oneness in family terms. Believers are brothers and sisters in Christ. This means believers must love each other as brothers and sisters (33–34). Yet it also means that when believers encounter one another in community, they are not encountering one another *directly*. They are encountering Jesus, the one who created the brothers and sisters and mediates peace between them in the community (34). He stands between them to reconcile them to him and to each other. Bonhoeffer claims, "We have one another only through Christ, but through Christ we really do *have* one another. We have one another completely and for all eternity" (34). Christ's mediation

> dismisses at the outset every unhappy desire for something more. Those who want more than what Christ has established between us do not want Christian community. They are looking for some extraordinary experiences of community that were denied them elsewhere. Such people are bringing confused and tainted desires into the Christian community. (34)

Bonhoeffer's insistence on the community's identity in Christ leads him to two key convictions about Christian communities. He considers it best for all members of the community to understand these. He writes, "It is essential for Christian community that two things become clear right from the beginning. *First, Christian community is not an ideal, but a divine reality; second, Christian community is a spiritual [pneumatische] and not a psychic [psychische] reality*" (35, italics original). Both points provide warnings against traits that destroy community.

The first point relates to the fact that, in Bonhoeffer's opinion, "On innumerable occasions a whole Christian community has been shattered because it has lived on the basis of a wishful image" (35). This is particularly true of "serious Christians who are put in a community for the first time," for they often have a distinct idea of what the community should be (35). These persons can quickly become very disillusioned with the community. They may wish to change it, critique it, or leave it. Any veteran faculty member, administrator, or staff member at a Christian university or seminary recognizes this person. So does any discerning student. Many of us were that person at one time.

Because of his grace, Christ does not allow us to persist in these illusionary images of the ideal community (35). "For God is not a

God of emotionalism, but the God of truth" (35). Therefore, he lets communities experience disillusionment. Bonhoeffer comments:

> Only that community which enters into the experience of this great disillusionment with all its unpleasant and evil appearances begins to be what it should be in God's sight, begins to grasp in faith the promise that is given to it. The sooner this moment of disillusionment comes over the individual and the community, the better for both. (35)

A community that does not deal with and grow from this disillusionment "loses at the same time the promise of a durable Christian community" (36).

Bonhoeffer had already experienced the difference between the ideal and the actual community in Finkenwalde, Köslin, and Gross Schlönwitz. The ideal student and faculty member found in *The Cost of Discipleship* did not always make an appearance. Students did not always stay. Bonhoeffer himself wished to get away. Grumbling happened. The Confessing Church disappointed. Visions of the future got crushed. These were God's gifts to bring the seminarians and their director into reality. All this reminds one of Jeremiah 11:18–12:6, where Jeremiah complains of his lot in life only to be told by God that times would get harder. It brings to mind Hebrews 10:36, where the author tells his readers, who have suffered plenty, they need more endurance.

God is gracious, and he cares for the character of each community member. Thus, he cannot allow an individual to insist on his or her vision of ideal community. As Bonhoeffer writes:

> God hates this wishful dreaming because it makes the dreamer proud and pretentious. Those who dream of this idealized community demand that it be fulfilled by God, by others, and by themselves. They enter the community of Christians with their demands, set up their own law, and judge one another and God accordingly. (36)

They become accusers of others, God, and themselves (36).

God calls us to a better way. Bonhoeffer emphasizes the importance of thankfulness to God for the community one has.

> Because God already has laid the only foundation of our community, because God has united us in one body with other Christians in Jesus Christ long before we entered into common life with them, we enter into that life together with other Christians, not as those who make demands, but as those who thankfully receive. (36)

Community life is inextricably linked with our salvation and incorporation into Christ's body. God had the community already in mind when he predestined each member for salvation and good works before he created the world (see Eph. 1:3–2:10). One should therefore be thankful for what God has done. One should be thankful in big and small things (37). One should stop complaining and start "letting our community grow according to the measure and riches that are there for us all in Jesus Christ" (37).

This attitude of thankfulness in the seminary community has a particular application to parish ministry. Bonhoeffer observes that pastors and keen church members often complain about the church. He then cautions, "Pastors should not complain about their congregations, certainly never to other people, but also not to God. Congregations have not been entrusted to them in order that they should become accusers of their congregations before God and their fellow human beings" (37). Pastors need to have their own illusions about churches shattered. When this happens, they must thank God that they are now living by faith anchored in reality rather than in their own dreams for a great church and a great ministry that will affirm them (38). After all, "Like the Christian's sanctification, Christian community is a gift of God to which we have no claim" (38). In summarizing this first key point, Bonhoeffer reminds readers, "Christian community is not an ideal we have to realize, but rather a reality created by God in Christ in which we may participate" (38).

Now Bonhoeffer moves to his second key principle. Since the

Christian community "is founded solely on Jesus Christ," it is a reality grounded in God's Spirit, not the human psyche (38). "In this respect it differs absolutely from all other communities" (38). This point, like the first, sets Christian communities apart from other organizations that may share some traits with them.

The Christian community's basis "is the clear, manifest Word of God in Jesus Christ" (39), while communities built on human spirit alone are based on "the dark, impenetrable urges and desires of the human soul" (39). The difference between the two types of communities is that of light and darkness (39). It is the difference between love and lust (39–40). It is the difference between communities built on God's Word and communities built on the power of charismatic leaders (40).

It is also the difference between *leaders* who want direct access to other persons, bypassing Christ, so that they can control others to reach their personal goals for the community or some individual, and *shepherds* who see Christ between them and others (40–41). Such leaders, as opposed to true shepherds of Christ and his body, are bent on bringing others into their sphere of influence (41). Bonhoeffer explains, "Here is where self-centered, strong persons enjoy life to the full, securing for themselves the admiration, the love, or the fear of the weak. Here human bonds, suggestive influences, and dependencies are everything" (41).

Such emotion-based approaches to community life are similar to emotion-based "conversion" and emotion-based "love" of neighbor (42). People who attach themselves to Christian communities because of a strong effect on their emotions often turn away when reality overtakes emotion. The same is true of solely emotion-based love of neighbor (42). When the neighbor does not respond to the person's vision, the person turns against the neighbor (43). Those who have solely emotion-based desires for community cannot bear to see the community dissolved (43). It must endure to make the dreamer's wishes come true.

Reality in Christ requires seeing Christ mediating between us and others (43). It demands that we let others have "the freedom to be Christ's" (44). This reality and freedom will be reflected in the daily life of work, family, and worship (46). In fact, if the community cannot see Christ in others in the hard work of day-to-day living, the community must take stock of the situation (47). Its members must turn from wishes to concrete daily life and all it means in Christ. To illustrate this point Bonhoeffer contrasts retreats and daily life in community. Because they are not bolted to daily reality, retreats are often the breeding ground of emotional, not spiritual, expectations (47). They do not offer the long perspective life requires and thrusts upon us. They are useful, yet must not be mistaken for real life.

In conclusion, Bonhoeffer notes that God has granted an uplifting experience to nearly everyone who has participated in true Christian community (47). He is opposed not to emotion, but to making emotion as he has defined it the guiding principle in community. This opening chapter of *Life Together* is fundamental to all that follows. One must accept the reality of the community established by God in Christ as seen in the lives of others. One must resist emotion-based and thus manipulative definitions of the community in favor of Spirit- and Word-based ones. Those who embrace these truths find Christ bringing unity, peace, and maturity in the community (47). Visible community rests in unseen realities, but the reality does not remain unseen. Such is God's gift and challenge of community.

Without the points Bonhoeffer has made about the nature of Christian community, the rest of the book will seem like a list of rules, however one reads what else he has written. If one views a seminary or other Christian ministry as something other than the reality of the body of Christ engaged in Spirit and Word ministry, one will find what follows optional. For instance, if one views a seminary as a place that only trains for tasks, transfers information, offers credentials, or sells the commodity of academic credits, then one will not see the need for time together in community. Time together will be a nice extracurricular addition for those who can participate, but not a necessary feature of the body of Christ. But if one accepts the concept of a seminary as the work of the body of Christ and thus as a visible work, then one will judge Bonhoeffer's statements on another level. One will then decide *how* best to conduct time together, not decide *whether* it is useful.

The Day Together

The daily spiritual exercises expected of all members of Finkenwalde created some controversy at the time. Bonhoeffer required silence before the morning service, which consisted of Bible reading, prayers, and hymns. He also required a time of silent meditation and intercession after breakfast before lectures began. The community also had a similar evening service, and at times readings during lunch. Though these exercises were balanced by study, lectures, and recreation, many objected to such "Catholic" practices. Others considered them evidences of legalism at Finkenwalde. Why did Bonhoeffer require these aspects of the community's day together and its day alone?

He did so because he believed that students were members of Christ's body preparing to be shepherds of the body of Christ. Therefore, they needed to learn more than they currently knew about how to read the Bible, listen to God, pray, and prepare for the rigors of ministry and persecution. They also needed to learn how to guide their churches into such spiritual family activities.

In a letter to Karl Barth dated September 19, 1936, Bonhoeffer explains his thinking.[14] He begins by stating how much he liked his assignment: "Work at the seminary gives me great joy. Academic and practical work are combined splendidly. I find that all along the line the young theologians coming into the seminary raise the very questions that have been troubling me recently, and of course our life together is strongly influenced by this."[15]

---

[14]I owe this connection between the letter to Barth and Bonhoeffer's educational-formational practices to *DBW* 5:121–22.

[15]Geffrey B. Kelly and F. Burton Nelson, eds., *A Testament to Freedom: The Essential Writings of Dietrich Bonhoeffer* (San Francisco: HarperCollins, 1990), 454. See also *DBW* 14:252–55.

Next, he comments on the necessity of the type of work he gives the students:

> I am firmly convinced that in view of what the young theologians bring with them from university and in view of the independent work which will be demanded of them in the parishes—particularly here in the East—they need a completely different kind of training which life together in a seminary like this unquestionably gives.[16]

Then, he asserts why he thinks such is the case: "You can hardly imagine how empty, how completely burnt out, most of the brothers are when they come to the seminary. Empty not only as regards theological insights and still more as regards knowledge of the Bible, but also as regards their personal life."[17]

Pressing his argument, he observes that he once heard Barth say that students often need someone to ask them how their souls are faring. Then he adds:

> The need has not been met since then, not even by the Confessing Church. But there are very few who recognize this sort of work with young theologians as a task of the church and do something about it. And it is really what everyone is waiting for. Unfortunately I am not up to it, but I remind the brothers of each other, and that seems to me to be the most important thing.[18]

Bonhoeffer continues by noting how such work on behalf of the students' souls unfolds: "It is, though, certain that both theological work and real pastoral fellowship can only grow in a life which is governed by gathering around the Word morning and evening and by fixed times of prayer."[19]

Finally, he addresses the charge of legalism. Frankly, he finds it absurd. "The charge of legalism does not seem to me to fit at

---

[16] Kelly and Nelson, *A Testament to Freedom*, 454.
[17] Ibid.
[18] Ibid.
[19] Ibid.

all. What is there legalistic in a Christian setting to work to learn what prayer is and in his spending a good deal of his time in this learning?"[20] He recounts the criticism of one Confessing Church brother:

> A leading man in the Confessing Church recently said to me, "We have no time for meditation now, the ordinands should learn how to preach and to catechize." That seems to me either a complete misunderstanding of what young theologians are like today or a culpable ignorance of how preaching and catechism come to life.[21]

In fact, Bonhoeffer claims:

> The questions that are seriously put to us today by young theologians are: How do I learn to pray? How do I learn to read the Bible? If we cannot help them there we cannot help them at all. And there is nothing really obvious about it. To say, "If someone does not know that, then he should not be a minister" would be to exclude most of us from our profession.[22]

Lest he be misunderstood, Bonhoeffer states that he is not emphasizing spiritual exercises to the exclusion of exegesis and theological reflection. He writes, "It is quite clear to me all these things are only justified when alongside them and with them—at just the same time!—there is really serious and sober theological, exegetical, and dogmatic work going on. Otherwise all these questions are given the wrong emphasis."[23] Bonhoeffer balances his demands for quality academic work with the needs of the community God has sent him. He does not wish for another type of student than those he has received. Yet he also balances the need for careful and strenuous thought and prayer. He does not believe a pastor can succeed in God's eyes without exegetical theology and biblical devotion.

These comments to Barth illuminate the second chapter of *Life*

---

20 Ibid.
21 Ibid.
22 Ibid.
23 Ibid., 454–55.

Together, which focuses on the time the community spends together in worship. Citing the fact that Christ arose from the dead in the morning, Bonhoeffer argues that day belongs to the risen Christ (48–49). Therefore, it is fitting for the Christian community to share in a worship service as the day begins (51). This practice is in keeping with that of many biblical characters who sought God in the morning (51–52). It is also anchored in the conviction that God has made the new day, which is a cause of great joy, and in the conviction that the Creator of the new day should have the first word in it (52). Before the anxieties and joys of daily life begin, the community has the gift of hearing the One who will be with them in all circumstances.

Bonhoeffer observes that different communities will have different ways of worshiping together in the morning. For instance, a community that includes children will not operate like one that does not (52). Still, every community worship service ought to include the word of Scripture, hymns of the church, and prayer based on the psalms (52–53). Since many churches have lost the practice of using the psalms, Bonhoeffer notes, it will be necessary to "recover the meaning of praying" them (53). This need remains in most places today, though some Christian communities make regular effective use of the psalms.

Having made this assertion about the psalms, Bonhoeffer explains how it is possible to pray them now. He observes that many people find it easy to pray psalms they understand (54). One could add that these psalms likely include psalms of joy, confession of sin, and specific petition. Yet it can be hard to know how to pray psalms that denounce enemies and affirm innocence (54). Bonhoeffer's solution is that believers should understand the psalms as the prayers of Jesus (54–55). Therefore, when the congregation, the body of Christ, prays the psalms, they are praying Jesus's prayers until he comes (55). Every word of the psalms is a prayer the community can pray because they are their Lord's prayers. Only in him can the community pray about enemies, friends, and forgiveness.

As the community prays the psalms, the members learn three

things. First, they learn that prayer means "praying on the basis of the Word of God, on the basis of promises. Christian prayer takes its stand on the solid ground of the revealed Word and has nothing to do with vague, self-seeking desires. We pray on the basis of the prayer of the truly human Jesus Christ" (55).

Second, the community learns "from the prayer of the Psalms what we should pray" (56). The psalms cover the whole realm of human experience. They even touch on vengeance. Bonhoeffer asserts that believers can pray these psalms "through and from the heart of Jesus," the one who took all God's vengeance on himself and still forgave his enemies (56). They can pray through Jesus because his heart was pure before God (56) and his suffering was as real as ours (56–57). Bonhoeffer advises that it is only possible for anyone to enter into such prayers gradually (57).

Third, praying the psalms helps believers "pray as a community" (57). Many psalms were originally prayed as community laments or praises, and some were sung or said antiphonally (57). It will take time for the community to pray as one, but the results repay the efforts (58).

Praying the psalms leads naturally into Bible reading. Bonhoeffer notes that 1 Timothy 4:13 calls believers to "give attention to the public reading of scripture." He then observes that he and many others "have grown up with the idea that the Scripture reading is solely a matter of hearing the Word of God for today. That is why for many Scripture reading consists only of a few selected verses that are to form the central idea of the day" (58). While he respects the value of such reading, Bonhoeffer finds it inadequate, for the "Holy Scriptures are more than selected Bible passages. . . . It is God's revealed Word for all peoples, for all times. The Holy Scriptures do not consist of individual sayings, but are a whole and can be used most effectively as such. The Scriptures are God's revealed Word as a whole" (59–60).

Practically speaking, this means the community needs to read the whole Bible, not just pieces of it. Bonhoeffer continues:

The full witness to Jesus Christ the Lord can be clearly heard only in its immeasurable inner relationships, in the connection of Old and New Testaments, of promise and fulfillment, sacrifice and law, Law and Gospel, cross and resurrection, faith and obedience, having and hoping. That is why daily worship together must include a longer Old and New Testament lesson besides the prayer of the Psalms. (60)

Bonhoeffer exclaims that surely a community of faith can read a chapter of the Old Testament and a half chapter of the New Testament (60).

He warns readers that there will opposition to this practice of longer readings, most likely because he experienced objections in the seminary community.[24] In response, he writes, "If it is really true that it is hard for us, as adult Christians, to comprehend a chapter of the Old Testament in its context, then that can only fill us with profound shame" (60). Such opposition merely shows the need to take Bibles in hand and begin to recover lost ground (60). He challenges seminarians to lead the way in this recovery and to stop making excuses: "And should not the seminarians be the very first to get to work here? Let us not argue that it is not the purpose of daily worship together to get to know the contents of Scripture, that it is too profane a purpose, something that must be achieved apart from daily worship" (60). Such objections amount to

a completely wrong understanding of what a daily worship service is. God's Word is to be heard by all in their own way and according to the measure of their understanding. A child hears and learns the biblical story for the first time during daily worship. Mature Christians keep on learning it and learn it better and better; and as they read and hear it on their own, they will never finish this learning. (60–61)

Part of this learning will occur as hearers of all ages hear the Bible's whole story, for the Bible is "a living whole" (61). Consecutive

---

[24] See Bethge, *DB*, 463.

Bible reading puts "the listening congregation in the midst of the wonderful revelatory world of the people of Israel" and draws them "into the Christmas story, the baptism, the miracles and discourses, the suffering, dying, and rising of Jesus Christ. It participates in the events that once occurred on this earth for the salvation of the whole world. In so doing, it receives salvation in Jesus Christ here and in all these events" (61–62). As the body of Christ, the community can claim they are part of the story. The Bible is not foreign subject matter. It is personal: "For those who want to hear, reading the biblical books in a sequential order forces them to go, and allow themselves to be found, where God has acted once and for all for the salvation of human beings" (62).

Such reading will once again remind the community of its roots. Salvation comes from outside the community; it comes from God. As Bonhoeffer confesses, "I find salvation not in my life story, but only in the story of Jesus Christ" (62). Help and guidance for living likewise come from outside the community; they come from the Bible. He writes: "Because it pleased God to act for us there, it is only there that we will be helped. Only in the Holy Scriptures do we get to know our own story. The God of Abraham, Isaac, and Jacob is the God and Father of Jesus Christ and our God" (62).

Such reading connects the community members to Reformation priorities and will enable ongoing ministry. Bonhoeffer claims that it is time to "get to know the Scriptures as the reformers and our forebears knew them" (63). Only then can a reforming body such as the Confessing Church have confidence for taking future steps (63). Only by such deep and broad absorption in the Bible can pastors rightly help others through God's Word, the only true help they can offer (63). Only Bible-saturated pastors and churches will find their appropriate God-given place in the world.

Praying the psalms and Bible reading naturally encourage the community to sing together. Bonhoeffer cites numerous biblical texts as evidence that the body of Christ ought to celebrate the opportunity to sing God's praises (65–66). Christ's body sings in heaven and on earth (65), and each "heart sings because it is filled with Christ" (66). Bonhoeffer was a good musician. He knew the difference between poor and excellent singing. He could have stressed many things regarding congregational singing.

Yet one thing is paramount in his mind: singing in unison. He asserts, "The essence of all congregational singing . . . is the purity of unison singing—untouched by the unrelated motives of musical excess . . . ; it is the simplicity and unpretentiousness, the humanness and warmth, of this style of singing" (67). Unison singing forces the singers to set aside individualistic desires for personal expression in favor of united praise to God. For Bonhoeffer "unison singing is much less a musical than a spiritual matter. Only where everybody in the community is prepared to assume an attitude of devotion and discipline can unison singing give us the joy that is its alone, even if it exhibits musical shortcomings" (67). As the community sings, it sings with the whole body of Christ on earth and in heaven; it does not sing alone (68).

After praying the psalms, reading the Bible, and singing, the community ends its service with an intercessory prayer. Bonhoeffer preferred that this prayer be extemporaneous and always offered by the same person. He offered this prayer as the director of the seminary. This assignment is not easy, so the one responsible must be ready to fulfill it humbly, even in times of personal emptiness, and the others must pray for this person (70). Extemporary prayer in this instance reflects the fact that each day has its own needs, and even a struggling prayer honors God's rule over the new day (71).

Once God has had the first word of the day, the community gathers for a meal. They gather with gratitude that God gives them their daily bread just as he has given them the bread of life (71–72). They eat together with joy over what the day brings, not simply with the expectation (or dread) of work to come (72–73). Life is "not only a great deal of trouble and hard work; it is also refreshment and joy in God's goodness" (73). This is especially important to remember as the community goes into the world to do its work.

Having begun the day with God one can do the work the world requires without self-absorption (75). Believers can achieve what is necessary and good in God's world in a spirit of prayer informed by the Bible and supported by others (75–76). If possible the community will meet for the midday meal to share thanks for God's provision, in faith that he will give them strength and success in their tasks and bring them together again by evening (77–78).

The day together closes with an evening worship time: "When night falls, the true light of God's word shines brighter for the community of faith. The prayer of the Psalms, a Scripture reading, a hymn, and a prayer close the day as they opened it" (78). Despite the similarity with the morning worship, however, Bonhoeffer identifies some special emphases at night. This is the time to give thanks for the day's blessings, the time to intercede for others as problems have arisen, and the time to ask forgiveness of sins committed that day against one another (78–80). This is the time to ask for protection, the time to make sure the community prays Psalm 74:16, "Yours is the day, yours also the night" (80).

Bonhoeffer's comments about praying the psalms, reading the Bible, singing hymns, and interceding for others do not just apply to a seminary community. Nonetheless, he tested these ideas in Finkenwalde and continued them in Köslin, Gross Schlönwitz, and Sigurdshof. They reflect his vision of a visible body of future pastors living as brothers in Christ so that they can later reform churches around similar practices for the same theological reasons. They respond to the needs he found in the students that he reported in his letters to Karl Barth and others.

His rationale for praying the psalms has received significant attention through the years. But his statements about Bible reading and hymn singing may need further exploration now and in the future. His insistence on reading longer pieces from every part of the Bible has not found acceptance in many seminaries or churches. Thus, students have not found themselves in the great stream of Christian history. Music has become increasingly individualistic in many places. The community's sense of praising God as a whole body is thereby diminished, as is the community's sense of being part of the unified body of Christ. Recapturing Bonhoeffer's vision of daily worship could instruct, inform, inspire, and unite seminary communities as they prepare ministers for the visible, united body of Christ.

The Day Alone

Bonhoeffer opens his chapter on the "day alone" with Psalm 65:1, a text that connects praise and silence (81). He then notes again that many people seek a Christian community for the wrong reasons. One is that they want to use the community as a spiritual sanatorium (81–82). We might say today that they want the community to be their therapy group. Such persons can be guilty of talking incessantly, almost as if they fear being alone. Bonhoeffer writes very severely about this problem, commenting, "Such attempts to find healing result in the undermining of speech and all genuine experience and, finally, resignation and spiritual death" (82). Given the fears that drive such people, Bonhoeffer states two principles around which he builds his comments in this chapter.

First, "*Whoever cannot be alone* [allein] *should beware of community*" (82, italics original). People who cannot be alone harm the community and misunderstand the Christian life. Bonhoeffer comments, "Alone you stood before God when God called you. Alone you had to obey God's voice. Alone you had to take up your cross, struggle, and pray and alone you will die and give an account to God. You cannot avoid yourself, for it is precisely God who has singled you out" (82). Therefore, he warns, "If you do not want to be alone, you are rejecting Christ's call to you, and you can have no part in the community of those who are called" (82).

Second, "the reverse is also true. *Whoever cannot stand being in community should beware of being alone*" (82, italics original). When God calls a person, he calls that person into the body of Christ, so he calls that person into an existing community.

A seminarian enters the community of those called to a shepherding role (82–83). In community a person must seek the good of others. Whereas persons afraid of being alone "want community without solitude" and "plunge into the void of words," it is also true that "those who seek solitude without community perish in the bottomless pit of vanity, self-infatuation, and despair" (83). Both types of problems can and must be avoided.

The way for both types of person to move forward is to embrace solitude within community. Bonhoeffer claims that the mark of solitude is silence, just as the mark of speech is the sign of community (83). He clearly has a high view of speech and community, given all that he has written in the chapter on the day together. But he also has a high view of the individual existing as a free and responsible person in the community. So he stresses the self-discipline of keeping silent for specific times during the day. He notes that these times of silence "will mainly be the times before and after hearing the Word. The Word comes not to the noisemakers but to those who are silent. The stillness of the temple is the sign of God's holy presence in the Word" (84). Though he does not cite Habakkuk 2:20 at this point, he may well have that text in mind. He does cite Ecclesiastes 3:7, which states that there is a time to speak and time to be silent (84).

There are reasons for observing silence after hearing the Word. Bonhoeffer believed it proper to let God have the first and last words of every day, so he emphasized the value of morning and evening worship (85). Furthermore, such silence gives people living together in a busy and noisy space the chance to think. It also gives them time for personal "clarification, purification, and focus on what is essential" (85). It gives them time to wait on God's Word and God's blessing (85).

Even in Bonhoeffer's day talk took priority over silence: "But everybody knows this is something that needs to be learned in these days when idle talk has gained the upper hand. Real silence, real stillness, really holding one's tongue, comes only as the sober consequence of spiritual silence" (85). Since this was Bonhoeffer's opinion in 1938, he would surely find silence even more precious in our current media-saturated world. Talk never stops now, not even when a person is alone. Indeed, people now have more ways of avoiding silence than ever.

Bonhoeffer believes that every Christian needs a daily time of silence for personal consideration of the Bible, for prayer, and for intercession (86). These are the purposes of meditation. "It serves no other purpose. Spiritual experiments have no place here" (86). Believers must take time for these "because it is precisely God who requires them of us. Even if for a long time meditation were to mean nothing but that we are performing a service we owe to God, this would be reason enough to do it" (86). By defining meditation as spending time in Scripture, prayer, and intercession, Bonhoeffer connects his ideas with what many of us are used to calling a personal devotional life. He is not advocating a synthesis with Eastern religions or an esoteric brand of Christianity.

One of the values of meditation is that it does not "allow us to sink into the void and bottomless pit of aloneness" (86). Rather, it puts us in contact with God's Word, which is "solid ground on which to stand and clear guidance for the steps we have to take" (87). Bonhoeffer suggests using shorter passages in meditation than those read in morning and evening worship (87). The longer passages offer breadth, while the shorter ones offer depth (87). The goal is to "expose ourselves to the particular sentence and word until we personally are affected by it" (87). He notes that other goals should not be pursued at this point. He writes, "For those of us who are preachers that means we will not ask how we should preach or teach on this text, but what it has to say to us personally" (87).

This does not mean the text will say something other than what the passage means, since "it is true that to do this we must first have understood the content of the text" (87). The community reading and theological lectures the seminarians experienced would help them understand the contents. It means that "we are rather waiting for God's word to us . . . we are waiting on the basis of a clear promise" (87). God's Word will come, so meditation begins with a prayer that God's Word will be heard and obeyed (87).

Bonhoeffer does not have unrealistic goals for meditation on the Bible. One does not have to think through the implications of every word or phrase. Some Bible concepts are too expansive to do this anyway (87–88). One does not have to come up with new ideas in meditation (88). Most of all, it is not necessary to have or expect to have great experiences in meditation (88). Desiring these puts one back into the realm of unreality and emotionalism. One need simply "pay attention to the Word alone and leave it to the Word to deal effectively with everything" (88). The goal is to seek God, not our own definition of "happiness" (89). After all, he observes, "If you seek God alone, you will gain happiness—that is the promise of all meditation" (89).

Thinking about the Bible naturally leads into prayer (89). Bonhoeffer again emphasizes that the "most promising way to pray is to allow oneself to be guided by the words of the Bible, to pray on the basis of the words of Scripture. In this way we will not fall prey to our own emptiness" (89). Prayer anchored in the Bible "means nothing else but the readiness to appropriate the Word, and what is more, to let it speak to me in my personal situation, in my particular tasks, decisions, sins, and temptations. What can never enter the prayer of the community may here silently be made known to God" (89). Prayer based in the Bible asks that it "may throw light on our day, preserve us from sin, and enable us to grow in holiness, and that we may be faithful in our work and have the strength to do it" (89). Bonhoeffer suggests that when our thoughts wander during prayer, we bring what comes to mind into the prayer (89).

Prayer for our own needs should naturally lead to intercession for others. Intercession should begin with the community of which we are a part, for a "Christian community either lives by the intercessory prayers of its members for one another, or the community will be destroyed" (90). In Bonhoeffer's opinion, intercessory prayer can overcome every cause of division and discord (90). Intercessory prayer "means nothing other than Christians bringing one another into the presence of God, seeing each other under the cross as poor human beings and sinners in need of grace. Then, everything about other people that repels me falls away" (90). In short, "Offering intercessory prayer means granting other Christians the same right we have received, namely, the right to stand before Christ and to share in Christ's mercy" (90–91).

Intercessory prayer is not a flight into the spiritual ether. It is concrete. It deals with "specific persons and specific difficulties and therefore specific requests. The more concrete my intercessory prayer becomes, the more promising it is" (91). It is service that we owe to God and one another (91); it is not a way to bask in our spiritual superiority. Because it is service to God, however, it is a source of true joy (91). Because it is service to God it is a gift of God (91). It is not drudgery assigned by a demanding God and done by an unwilling servant.

Though all Christians should be involved in the three aspects of meditation, pastors have a particular biblical responsibility to practice them. For it is the pastor "on whom the needs of the whole community of faith rest" (91). Thus, pastors must develop the discipline necessary for daily time in meditation (91). This is not legalism. It is biblical faithfulness (91). As Bonhoeffer concludes, "For the pastor it is an indispensable duty on which the whole practice of ministry will depend. Who can really be faithful in great things, if they have not learned to be faithful in the things of daily life?" (91).

As he closes this chapter, Bonhoeffer unites the individual and the community again. He combines the day together and the day alone. Quite rightly he observes that Christians often spend many hours of every day alone in "an unchristian environment. These are times of *testing*" (91). As such, they are the times in which it becomes evident whether the community has "served to make individuals free, strong, and mature, or has it made them insecure and dependent?" (91–92). Community life and meditation should make the individual strong for the times of testing. Community life and meditation should lead them to be ready for the reality of the daily world, not give them momentary escape from that reality (92).

Whatever one does in community or in solitude affects the whole community. Bonhoeffer writes, "Every act of self-discipline by a Christian is also a service to the community. Conversely, there is no sin in thought, word, or deed, no matter how personal or secret, that does not harm the whole community" (92). This is true because the community is the body of Christ: "Every member serves the whole body, contributing either to its health or to its ruin, for we *are* members of one body not only when we want to be, but in our whole existence" (92). Bonhoeffer warns, "This is not a theory, but a spiritual reality that is often experienced in the Christian community with shocking clarity, sometimes destructively and sometimes beneficially" (92). The goal is for every day alone to end as every day together does, which is with joy and the willingness to forgive others. It is for every person to have found God's strength equal for every challenge (92).

As time passed, Bonhoeffer's students increasingly saw the value of meditation, as did Bonhoeffer. For instance, Hans-Werner Jensen writes:

> Professor Schniewind of Kiel, by pointing to the prayers of the Baltic martyrs, had started me on the way which in Gross Schlönwitz led to clarity of conviction: I saw the meaning of the psalms as the prayers of the Church, of the people of God, in the desert. I was happy to learn this in the Preachers' Seminary, for I was able to practice it later in a Gestapo prison.[25]

Bethge notes that when Bonhoeffer was imprisoned, he continued his practice of meditation and was glad he had learned so many

---

[25] In *I Knew Dietrich Bonhoeffer*, ed. Wolf-Dieter Zimmermann and Ronald Gregor Smith, trans. Kathe Gregor Smith (New York: Harper and Row, 1966), 153.

hymns by heart.[26] Terrible times showed the value of what some of Bonhoeffer's first seminarians initially opposed.[27]

In some ways this chapter on the day alone is even more central to Bonhoeffer's vision for theological education than his description of life together. After all, few pastors are able to continue all the practices of the seminary's day together in their parishes, though some may be able to do so. I am aware, for instance, of Anglican pastors who meet together for Morning Prayer daily. But every pastor has responsibilities that are wed to time alone. The Bible gives pastors the tasks of prayer, teaching, intercession, and feeding on God's Word. As Bonhoeffer has indicated, the burdens of the whole congregation fall on the pastor. Yet pastors are also sinners in need of grace. Their strength must come from God, and God gives the Bible, prayer, and intercession as means of grace for the pastor and the congregation. Learning how to appropriate this great gift is a worthy pursuit for the whole seminary community.

Service

As has been noted above, the Confessing Church sought to establish pastoral ministry on the basis of brotherhood instead of on privilege and prominence. This was a noble goal, and not one easily or always reached, as Bonhoeffer was well aware. For him, service—the topic of his next chapter—was the essential component in achieving that goal.

Bonhoeffer begins by citing Luke 9:46, which depicts a dispute among the disciples over which one of them was the greatest, the most important (93). He observes that everyone knows who sows such discord among Christians, yet Bonhoeffer notes that "perhaps we do not think enough about the fact that no Christian community ever comes together without this argument appearing as a seed of discord. No sooner are people together than they begin to observe, judge, and classify each other" (93). So it is imperative for their

---

[26] Bethge, *DB*, 852.
[27] On some of the students' opposition to meditation, see Wolf-Dieter Zimmermann's comments in Zimmermann and Smith, *I Knew Dietrich Bonhoeffer*, 109–10.

health that the community "keep an eye on this dangerous enemy from the very outset and eradicate it" (93). One could hope that such competitive instincts have been tamed in pastoral candidates. The sad truth is that ministers often compare themselves to other ministers, and this process begins or is enflamed in seminary.

Some basic principles will help the community combat this problem. First, community members can commit to not speaking about another person in secret (94). Bonhoeffer mentions James 4:11–12 and Ephesians 4:29 as reasons for this prohibition (94–95). Second, the community members can strive to let others be free creations. God made each person, and "God does not want me to mold others into the image that seems good to me, into my own image" (95). Third, the community members can recognize the value of each person and give each person a job to do so that even a weak member can have dignity and evident value to the community (95–96). Fourth, the community members can recall that justification comes from outside, from Jesus Christ, not through self-justification. Fifth, the community members can adopt the apostle's Paul's attitude of "considering oneself the worst of sinners" (97; see 1 Tim. 1:15).

Each of these principles leads to a single goal, which is to serve others. Once community members strive to serve others, they will no longer see the community as the place "in which they can most successfully promote themselves, but the place where they can best carry out their service" (95). With these cautions in place, Bonhoeffer proceeds to discuss the best four ways to serve others in a community of faith. His list is surprising in its simplicity.

Listening to others is the first act of service he describes. Bonhoeffer writes, "Just as our love for God begins with listening to God's word, the beginning of love for other Christians is learning to listen to them" (98). Similarly, prayer indicates that God listens to us; he does not just speak to us (98). We should follow his example. Preachers are particularly prone to talking, to feeling they must always have a word to say in all situations. So they must take time to learn how to listen (98). Bonhoeffer observes that those who do not listen to other believers are just as likely not to listen to God. He then warns, "The death of the spiritual life starts here, and in the end there is nothing left but empty spiritual chatter and clerical condescension which chokes on pious words. Those who cannot listen long and patiently will always be talking past others, and finally no longer will even notice it" (98). Failure to listen is, in effect, an unwillingness to hear anyone else. It is sheer selfishness born of the desire to pursue only one's own words and plans (98).

Bonhoeffer practiced such listening, but doing so did not necessarily come naturally. Johannes Goebel, a student in the first group at Zingst/Finkenwalde in 1935, later recalled how carefully Bonhoeffer listened to students. Goebel writes:

> Now in retrospect it seems to me that he did not come by it easily, that he even forced himself to it. At that time the deliberate self-effacement which he practiced in listening to us, but which involved a real and forceful transmission of strength, had an exciting effect on us, compelling us to the last effort, but at the same time liberating and relaxing us.[28]

Albrecht Schönherr, also a student in the first group and a founding member of the Brothers' House, likewise remembered that Bonhoeffer "took great trouble with those who were in real spiritual need, and had endless discussions with them and was ready to help them to the point of self-sacrifice."[29]

Active helpfulness is the second act of service he recommends. Every person in the community ought to be willing to do the tasks it takes to keep the community running. Bonhoeffer bluntly states: "Nobody is too good for the lowest service. Those who worry about the loss of time entailed by such small, external acts of helpfulness are usually taking their own work too seriously. We must be ready to allow ourselves to be interrupted by God" (99). Our time is not our own; God determines our schedule (100). Bonhoeffer's students and colleagues testify that he gave such service, whether it was

---

[28] Ibid., 124.
[29] See ibid., 128.

through spending time with them, visiting them in their parishes,[30] visiting them in prison,[31] or getting them better care at a hospital.[32]

Bearing with one another is the third act of service. Christians must put up with one another's quirks and failures. They must suffer with and endure one another (100). This is particularly hard in a community where everyone spends a lot of time together. Thus, it is important to treat the other person as "a brother or sister and not just an object to be controlled" (100). It is also important to admit that people are a heavy burden at times; indeed people are so heavy a burden that God sent Jesus to the cross to bear this burden (100–101). Their freedom is particularly a burden at times, for it affects us (101). Yet it was through carrying this burden of humanity that God maintained community with humanity (101). As community members view their bearing with one another as a reflection of the cross, the weak can learn to bear with the strong and the strong to bear with the weak (101–2). They can learn to offer forgiveness to others as Christ has offered forgiveness to them (102–3).

It is only as the first three acts of service are performed that the fourth act of service, the speaking of God's Word to others, can be offered effectively (103). As has been noted above, many pastors jump into speaking too quickly. They must learn to listen, help, and forbear. Yet the opposite is also true. Some community members find it hard to speak out. They may fear others too much to tell them the truth (103–4). They may not want responsibility for their brother, or they may fear addressing a stronger person (104).

Such concerns must be overcome. Each community member needs personal encouragement and correction. It is unchristian to withhold godly words that will help others (104). Every person needs God's comfort and admonition from another believer, even if expressed poorly (105). Every person needs discipline; it is not compassionate to let others continue in error. As Bonhoeffer argues:

---

[30] As Wolfgang Schrader, a student from the first course (1935), mentions in ibid., 149.

[31] Wilhelm Rott, inspector of students at Finkenwalde, recounts such a visit during 1937 in ibid., 135.

[32] As Hans-Werner Jensen, a student in the eighth course (1938–1939), recalls in ibid., 152.

Nothing can be more cruel than that leniency which abandons others to their sin. Nothing can be more compassionate than the severe reprimand which calls another Christian in one's community back from the path of sin. When we allow nothing but God's word to stand between us, judging and helping, it is a service of mercy, an ultimate offer of genuine community. (105)

This fourth service gives substance to Bonhoeffer's emphasis on hearing and forgiving. One does not merely put up with whatever another community member does simply because each member is God's creation. One helps shape the fellow believer through God's Word as needed. The goal is to hear and help and forbear first before speaking. Restraint and courage are therefore both needed.

Mark 10:43 provides the summation of this chapter: "Whoever wishes to be great among you must be your servant" (106). True spiritual authority exists only where real service exists. False spiritual authority contaminates. In one of the strongest statements in the book, Bonhoeffer writes, "Every personality cult that bears the mark of the distinguished qualities, outstanding abilities, powers, and talents of an other, even if these are of a thoroughly spiritual nature, is worldly and has no place in the Christian community of faith; indeed, it poisons the community" (106).

So why do so many people long for powerful, charismatic leaders in churches? According to Bonhoeffer, this desire "often enough stems from a spiritually sick need to admire human beings and to establish visible human authority because the genuine authority of service appears to be too insignificant" (106). This desire runs counter to Paul's standards for a bishop found in 1 Timothy 3 (106), and counter to Jesus's statement in Matthew 23:8 that the disciples have one teacher and they are all brothers (107).

The church must take the path Jesus and Paul require. Bonhoeffer asserts that service and faithfulness must be the earmarks of the church's shepherds: "The community of faith does not need brilliant personalities but faithful servants of Jesus and of one another. It does not lack the former, but the latter" (107). He concludes,

"The community of faith will place its confidence only in the simple servant of the Word of Jesus, because it knows that it will then be guided not by human wisdom and human conceit, but by the Word of the Good Shepherd" (107). Such shepherds know that their authority comes from God, not from talent that outshines all other competitors for notoriety and power.

Being overly influenced by a single individual student or teacher is always a danger in a seminary community. Bonhoeffer could have used his own considerable talent to force students into his mold. He could have done so almost without trying, so it is important to note that his students and colleagues report he consciously avoided this pitfall. Albrecht Schönherr recalled, "Bonhoeffer detested binding men to himself; perhaps for that very reason so many were drawn to him."[33] Hans-Werner Jensen, a student from the eighth session (1938–1939), adds that it "was not a naïve but a highly conscious love of the Christian community which drove Dietrich Bonhoeffer to become the father, pastor and neighbor of his seminarists. . . . He avoided keeping others in tutelage; he only wanted to help them."[34] Bonhoeffer was no more flawless in this area of service than he was in any other. Nonetheless, in our current age in which many pastors, seminary teachers, and seminary administrators compete for prominence, marketing themselves and their ministries as commodities, it is good to know that Bonhoeffer may have practiced what he preached.

Confession and the Lord's Supper

Bonhoeffer's last chapter covers one of the most difficult matters he asked of his seminarians: confessing sins to one another. As is his practice in *Life Together*, Bonhoeffer begins with a Bible verse, in this instance James 5:16, "Confess your sins to one another." He then links his emphasis on community to confession of sin by claiming:

---

[33] See ibid., 126.
[34] See ibid., 152.

Those who remain alone with their evil are left utterly alone. It is possible that Christians may remain lonely in spite of daily worship, prayer together, and all their community through service—that the final breakthrough to community does not occur precisely because they enjoy community with one another as pious believers, but not with one another as those lacking piety, as sinners. (108)

The community of faith truly becomes a community by loving one another as sinners *and* as faithful ones. By forgiving confessed sins the community does Christ's work as Christ's body (108–9).

There are at least four great benefits to confessing sins to one another, according to Bonhoeffer. There is a "breakthrough to community" as "the last stronghold of self-justification is abandoned" (110). There is a "breakthrough to the cross" as confession "deals a terrible blow to one's pride" and as the other person bears with the sins confessed (111). There is a "breakthrough to new life" as the believer renounces sin and gains Christ's victory over it (112). There is a "breakthrough to assurance" that comes from receiving Christ's forgiveness instead of self-forgiveness, and from receiving the promise of pardon from another (112–13).

Bonhoeffer notes some cautions about confession. Though confession is an act of community, only one person needs to hear another's confession. The one can act for the many (110). Also, though confession includes general admissions of sin, one should confess concrete sins. Confession should not be evasion. The Ten Commandments may serve as a guide in this area (113). Furthermore, though confession is commanded, it is not a law to be observed, but a grace to be received (114). Finally, though confession releases one's conscience, it is not a form of therapy. It is an experience of the cross (114–15). Indeed, when the community understands hearing confession as an act of cross bearing, "they will lose the spirit of human judgmentalism, as well as weak indulgence, receiving instead the spirit of divine firmness and divine love" (116).

Finally, two dangers should be avoided. First, one person should not hear everyone else's confessions. Doing so would be a tremendous burden for a single individual and could also lead to the temptation "to the unholy misuse of confession for the exercise of spiritual tyranny over souls" (116). Second, those who confess must not make confession into "a work of piety" (116). Doing so would make God's gift of life through forgiveness into an act of self-serving spiritual death (116).

Confession may occur as needed in the community, but perhaps its main value is "as a preparation for participation together in the *Lord's Supper*" (117). Confession leading to forgiveness will keep believers from coming to the service at odds with a brother or sister (117; see Matt. 5:23–24). Such confession transcends an apology (118) and will allow the community to come to the Lord's Table rejoicing in unity and wholeness (118). All the community's worship, meditation, and service culminate there, where the visible body of Christ receives community afresh in anticipation of life together throughout eternity (118). Bonhoeffer concludes, "Here the community has reached its goal. Here joy in Christ and Christ's community is complete. The life together of Christians under the Word has reached its fulfillment in the sacrament" (118).

Seen one way, the book concludes rather abruptly at this point, for Bonhoeffer introduces the Lord's Supper but does not deal with it. Seen another way, the ending is superb, since Bonhoeffer leaves the community of faith he has been describing at one with one another at the Lord's Table, waiting for the kingdom of God. Perhaps that is how Bonhoeffer envisioned his students and friends as he put down his pen. Like so many things related to Bonhoeffer, one cannot know for sure. Regardless, it is hard to think of a better ending for a volume dedicated to preserving a cross-bearing community in a harsh world.

Observations for Incarnational Seminaries Today

The Cost of Discipleship expresses what sort of students and faculty should constitute seminaries that are communities of costly grace that emphasize God's grace, God's call, God's standards for shepherds, and God's identification of the body of Christ. *Life Together* describes what Bonhoeffer wanted these communities of Christ's body to do together and explains briefly why he wanted them to do it. It would be very easy to focus on the former and ignore the latter. One can debate practices forever. To do so, however, would be to miss Bonhoeffer's main point. He was not out to establish a new brand of Protestant monasticism in Germany. The means mattered to him, and he kept students practicing them, but he linked these means to the end result, which mattered most to him. Bonhoeffer was trying to shape shepherds for local church communities of costly grace. Such pastors needed to understand how to preach, pray, read the Bible, serve the people of God, and live in family-type community with other believers. He believed that seminaries that formed such persons are special visible ministries of the body of Christ. He thought these communities should strive to reach at least three goals.

The Proper Grounds for an Incarnational Community

His first goal was to form *a community* on *proper grounds*. This community would be like the one Jesus formed with his disciples, described in *The Cost of Discipleship*. It would exist to shape shepherds who in turn help churches develop into communing brothers and sisters in Christ. Daily worship, prayer, and meditation were means of shaving off remaining edges of selfishness, ambition, wrongheaded individualism, and theological arrogance. When used this way, these practices helped students stop longing for a community to be a selfish psychological crutch or longing for solitude to the exclusion of others. Seminarians needed to understand the proper grounds of community so they could aid congregations in doing the same. Everything in ministry, from preaching to pastoral care, would thereby benefit.

Today we must ask ourselves if forming seminary communities for the purpose of shaping biblical churches is a conviction or a preference. Every seminary no doubt at least prefers for this to be one by-product of its work. But if it is a conviction, it will shape admissions, faculty recruitment and development, fundraising, curricular development, and cocurricular activities such as chapel, mentoring groups, student life, lectureships, and special events. Prospective students will be told that theology determines practice, that receiving personal therapy and reaching personal academic or ecclesiological career goals do not drive the seminary, and that caring for others is an expectation, not an option. Students, faculty, and staff will gladly embrace life together through common worship, prayer, burden bearing, and even hearing confession as needed. These will not be optional experiences, and they will not be done flawlessly or seamlessly. Those who do not wish to share in this ethos should not join the community. Students, faculty, and staff will also know that they will have positive time alone. Their personalities will not be set aside, but honored. There will be time to think, read, serve, recreate, and relate. They will not be expected to lose themselves as they serve the community.

Discipline will be needed to form such a community. Granting too many exceptions in admissions and too many exemptions from daily community life creates a protest group (quiet or not) that undermines community. Each community can decide how often to meet and how to care for one another. I believe Bonhoeffer would think each community is free to take the steps it deems appropriate. But each group will need some explanation, encouragement, and enforcement, lest grace and freedom become laziness, license, or self-indulgence in academics or entertainment. He was certainly willing to take such preventive steps.

Bible-Formed Shepherds in Churches and Seminaries

Bonhoeffer's second goal was to send out pastors who were Bible formed and thus able to pray, preach, humbly confess sins and hear others do the same, offer pastoral care, and be a brother or sister to other believers in church communities. Such persons obey God. As Wolf-Dieter Zimmermann, a student in the third course at Finkenwalde, noted, the seminarians were to learn that the Bible is not simply a subject to be "dissected into different sources and layers. The power of the word, just as it is transmitted, is only felt by him who bows before that word."[35] In short, Bonhoeffer desired to shape servants of the Lord Jesus Christ. He had no desire to produce denominational operators, or even what today's American culture defines as "visionary leaders." This desire required teaching every community member to work, and to work at whatever needed doing. It required that everyone hear long portions of God's Word, study theology closely, meditate on short portions of the Bible, hold his tongue, intercede for others, and share in the Lord's Supper. It required setting aside competition with others and the longing for, or to be, "leaders" defined by nonbiblical standards. The means are all related to the goal.

In my opinion few areas of seminary life today need more revision than what normally passes under the title of "leadership development." It is hard to find biblical passages that call for "leadership" in anything approximating what that term implies in American life. Models for pastors as chief executive officers or community activists do not exist in the Bible. To find them there, one has to begin with such concepts of leadership and then try to tie Bible verses to them in a noncontextual or barely contextual way. Pastors whose goal is to brand their ministries, build their reputations, manage a complex organization, become popular enough or singular enough to have off-site video churches, command six-figure book contracts for products mainly ghostwritten, and have thousands of followers on social media outlets do not match anything in the Pastoral Epistles. They match the "super apostles" who opposed Paul in Corinth.[36] A pastor may need to do some of these things, but if he cannot do them as a Bible-formed, praying servant of a community, he is not on the right path.

The same is true of seminary faculty and administration. Semi-

---

[35] Ibid., 108.

[36] I owe this insight and many others in this portion of the book to conversations with my friend Bruce Winter, former warden of Tyndale House, Cambridge, and principal of Queensland Theological College, Brisbane, and to the writings on 2 Corinthians by my friend Scott Hafemann.

naries are part of a very small and virtually unnoticed slice of American education. There is no real power to be gained from becoming a "great leader" along the lines established by American culture. Seminary teaching and administrating is service, pure and simple. These provide a prime opportunity to die to self. Seminary faculty and administration must avoid embodying the old joke that says the battles in academe over position, prestige, and office space are so vicious because the stakes are so low.

It is probably quixotic to suggest that *leadership* is a word not worth using to describe pastoral work. Nonetheless, at the very least the word *servant* must be prefaced to it. Many fine university and seminary colleagues I have now and have had in the past understand and teach this point. It is worth recalling that Paul asks people to imitate him as he imitates Christ, and to follow Jesus, not any human leader (1 Cor. 1:10–17; 11:1). Jesus comments that believers have one leader, one Lord, and that is Jesus Christ himself (Matt. 23:8). The Confessing Church was correct to assert that pastors need to be brothers and sisters, not lords, to one another and to their congregations.

A Visible Example of the Body of Christ

Bonhoeffer's third goal was to have a seminary that provided a visible example of the body of Christ. The body of Christ does the will of the Father in heaven. It worships him; it listens to his Word; it does the daily work of learning and serving; it prays to him for one another; it cares in person for each person, whether that means speaking or being silent; it uses its gifts wisely; it accepts support from those who love it; it offers hospitality to others; it goes about its daily work and returns to meet again; and it spreads the gospel of redemption in Jesus Christ beyond its boundaries. One could add to this list, but the point is clear: the body of Christ takes up positive space in the world. It seeks the face of others because it seeks the face of God. It sees the face of God in the face of others (see Matt. 25:31–46) as it waits to see Jesus face-to-face.

This visible nature of the seminary community appears in many places, but Bonhoeffer focuses on the community's life together in worship. His vision for this worship is regular, simple, Word-centered, musical, prayerful, required, and formational. It does not give a forum for famous pastors the seminary has invited because their recommendations can help seminary enrollment. It does not allow musicians to showcase their skills at the expense of common singing. It is not a place for professors to give another lecture. It believes that a seminary community can surely listen to a chapter and a half of Bible reading and not get irritated, as if hearing God's Word is less practical and important than voicing our own ideas. It believes that every community member needs to make a reasonable commitment to be there together, for the seminary is a familial community, not a place where classes, people, and worship run on parallel tracks.

Conclusion

These three goals are interconnected. A community cannot reach the third goal if it neglects the first two, unless by God's grace such happens without the seminary's help. If seminaries recruit students, staff, and faculty by promising to make them great individuals able to meet their own individualistic professional goals, they will have a hard time achieving any semblance of community or servants of Christ and his body. If seminaries offer classes at times of the day and in block formats that eliminate the likelihood of students, faculty, and staff engaging in personal relationships and corporate worship, they should not be surprised to encounter selfish pastors leading the churches they and their loved ones attend. They should not be surprised to find that such pastors encourage church members to treat "choosing a church," especially their church, like choosing any other consumable commodity. After all, their seminary experience helped train them to think like consultants and organizers, not humble servants of the body of Christ.

But there is no reason to end this chapter on a negative note.

After all, Bonhoeffer exits *Life Together* with the community observing the Lord's Supper, something the seminaries did once a month. The Lord's Supper is a moving, hope-filled sacrament. This conclusion reminds us that the community that has spent the day together and the day alone well by serving others and forgiving one another is a joyful group. It will send out members to change what needs changing in churches and reinforce what is good in them. This community's eating of the Lord's Supper is a down payment on the kingdom of God because it is the natural visible act of the functioning body of Christ. It is real, and it is beautiful. And it will last forever.

5

Visible Faithful Witnesses

The Seminary and Perseverance

The longing for God's word is distinguished, not by the heat of piety, but by the perseverance to the Word until the end.

Dietrich Bonhoeffer (1940)

Introduction

Both *The Cost of Discipleship* and *Life Together* express the difficult path of pastoral and seminary ministry. Each also relates the joy associated with the means and ends of conducting such ministries. The conditions under which they were written also reveal the challenges specifically associated with being a seminary educator. By the time Bonhoeffer finished writing *Life Together*, seven groups of seminarians had been sent out from Finkenwalde, Köslin, and Gross Schlönwitz. These former students were learning firsthand how hard ministry could be. Bonhoeffer himself was also discovering increasingly how rigorous the life of a seminary director and teacher, author, church resource person, and church reformer could be. Meanwhile, the eighth group of students stood ready to find out how tough being a seminary student could be. Local church and

seminary ministries are not easy today, much less under the circumstances Bonhoeffer, his students, and former students experienced.
Each one of these roles required then, and each requires now, singular faithfulness and perseverance. The Bible indicates that these
assignments cannot be fulfilled any other way.

This chapter focuses on how Bonhoeffer and his seminary ministry provided a visible example of faithfulness to his students, to
his former students, and to himself. It will note that Bonhoeffer
attempted to offer ongoing ministry to former students while continuing to prepare current students for what he and his former students were encountering in ministry. It will also chart Bonhoeffer's
own journey in knowing how to persevere in faithfulness to his
call to serve the Confessing Church through directing the seminary.
Then it will suggest ways seminaries today can provide the sort of
testimony of faithfulness that requires a personal, incarnational
basis.

To try to achieve these goals, I will first survey a wider range of
written materials than I did in the previous two chapters. This is
necessary, I think, because there is no completed published work
like *The Cost of Discipleship* or *Life Together* from this final period
of Bonhoeffer's seminary ministry (1938–1940). But this is not to
say the writings from this era are merely fragments from his life.
To the contrary, many of them are short gems devoted to specific
sequential aspects of the enduring, faithful life of Christian service,
which should be the goal of every seminary student, faculty member, staff member, and graduate.

I will then conclude this chapter with a discussion of Bonhoeffer's *Meditations on Psalm 119*, a piece that I believe is summative,
substantive, and beautiful in many ways. It reflects the personal
and ecclesiastical struggles he experienced in these years, and it
expresses what he learned from them. Though not exegetical in
the traditional sense of the term, the piece represents Bonhoeffer's
profound commitment to the Bible at this time and includes some
strategic insights into biblical discipleship. Sadly, it is unfinished,

ceasing after verse 21. At least there are no more handwritten pages. Apparently Bonhoeffer stopped there as the last term he would teach ended.

One can mourn the loss of further writing on this key psalm due to Bonhoeffer's loss of seminary ministry and eventually his untimely death. Or one can be more positive. Perhaps Bonhoeffer left the work expecting to come back to it in the future. Perhaps he was thinking like John Calvin, who was expelled from Geneva in 1538, then returned in 1541 and resumed preaching a text where he had left off before his exile. Regardless, this unfinished work stands as a testimony to faithfulness in harsh conditions, a trait Bonhoeffer and his students learned well and passed on to us today. They discovered they were on a path born of Christ's call in their lives, and only faithfulness keeps one on that path. Expressing this truth to students, alumni, and broader communities today must be part of the incarnational seminary's mission.

The Path of Faithfulness: 1937–1939

Bonhoeffer's writings during 1937–1939 emphasize again and again the need for the Confessing Church and thus for his former and current students to persevere on the path God had called them to follow. He found endurance so important for good reasons. By the time he finished writing *Life Together* in early October 1938, Bonhoeffer was already a tired young man.[1] It is hard to conceive that he, his colleagues, and anyone in a similar situation could be otherwise. He had been teaching, writing, directing the seminary, helping churches, traveling back and forth to Berlin regularly, and supporting former students now in ministry or seeking a ministry. The frenetic pace may have been at least partly fueled by the knowledge that any and all parts of this work could come to an end at any time. The routine he had established by now was challenging, to say the least.

---

[1] On this point, see Bethge, *DB*, 588–96; and Schlingensiepen, *DB*, 221–22.

Seminary Directing and Teaching:
Sixth, Seventh, and Eighth Groups (1937–1939)

The shift from Finkenwalde to Köslin and Gross Schlönwitz was made, and the new session, the sixth Bonhoeffer led, began by December 5, 1937, ending in late April 1938. The move required relocating Bonhoeffer, Bethge, and Onnasch and making arrangements for sixteen students. Bonhoeffer continued his normal lectures on the Bible, ecclesiology, and preaching, and he also gave lectures on pastoral counseling that have been preserved in outline form.[2] Though in a new venue, the teaching and community life did not change drastically in aim or in content.

For example, in a sermon delivered at Gross Schlönwitz dated January 23, 1938, Bonhoeffer expounded Romans 12:17–21 in manner very reminiscent of his statements on Matthew 5:43–48 in *The Cost of Discipleship*. The passage commands peace with others and not taking revenge on enemies, but rather letting God deal with the wicked. Bonhoeffer states that such peace with enemies comes only through extending the love of the cross to one's enemies (467). God has already taken vengeance by placing his judgment on Jesus (470). As believers refuse to respond to evil in kind, "the evil hits emptiness and finds nothing on which it can ignite" (471). Bonhoeffer then asks: "How do we overcome evil? By forgiving without end. How does that happen? By seeing the enemy as he truly is, the one for whom Christ died, the one whom Christ loved" (471).

Bonhoeffer also preached on the costs and joys associated with Christian faith in a sermon on Romans 5:1–5 delivered March 9, 1938, in Gross Schlönwitz (471). In this message he stressed how peace with God allows believers to rejoice in affliction. Those who are at peace with God are part of the church, and for the people Christ's "cross has become the eternal source of joy and hope in the coming glory of God" (473). How do believers know if they have this peace? Bonhoeffer asserts, "Whether we have truly found the

---

[2] See *DBW* 15:307–21. Unless otherwise noted, all subsequent quotations from Bonhoeffer's writings are from *DBW* 15, and page numbers are noted parenthetically.

peace of God will be proven by the way we deal with the afflictions that come upon us" (473). He notes that some people bow before the cross, yet show they actually hate the cross by refusing to accept affliction in their lives (473). They have sought peace with the world, not with God through the cross (473). They have sought personal peace in a way that shows they *use* the cross instead of loving it (473).

Love of the cross is essential for the Confessing Church, according to Bonhoeffer. He does not think the Confessing Church has had an easy path, for he writes, "Our church has suffered great affliction during the last few years: destruction of its order, the incursion of false proclamation, much enmity, evil words and slander, imprisonment and distress of all kinds, up to this very hour. And nobody knows what afflictions lie ahead for the church" (473–74). This situation makes it imperative that the church decide "whether we have peace with God or whether we have so far lived in an entirely worldly peace" (474). He then gets very specific:

> How much murmuring and resisting, how much contradiction and hatred against affliction has been uncovered among us. How much denying, standing on the sidelines, how much fear when the cross of Jesus began to overshadow only a small portion of our personal life! How often did we think that we could preserve our peace with God and at the same time still avoid suffering, renunciation, venom, and the endangerment of our existence! (474)

In clear, forceful, and pastoral terms Bonhoeffer thus addresses the Confessing Church's need to stand against all the forces arrayed against it.

Then he turns to how affliction produces patient endurance, or experience. To be patient is "to remain below, not to throw off the load but to bear it"—in fact, to stay under the load and not collapse under it (474). Remaining beneath the load requires "not giving up weakly . . . but under the burden gaining strength as a grace by God and preserving the peace of God without being shaken. The peace of God is with the patient ones" (475). To the patient ones, God sends trials and afflictions, so many in fact that at times they must "scream for the peace of God" (475). And God hears and sustains those who scream. He gives them hope, and this hope never leads to disgrace (475). As long as the church maintains this hope, all is well; when it loses this hope, all is lost (475).

Bonhoeffer concludes the sermon by returning to the theme of peace with God that flows from the love of God. Affliction, trial, and endurance are not ultimately what sustain believers. Rather, God's love undergirds the whole Christian life. Bonhoeffer concludes:

> Whomever it is granted by God through the Holy Spirit that the incomprehensible happens within him, namely, that he begins to love God for the sake of God and not for the sake of earthly goods and gifts, nor for the sake of peace, but truly and only for the sake of God, whomever the love of God in the cross of Jesus Christ befalls so that he begins to love God for the sake of Jesus Christ, whomever [sic] is led through the Holy Spirit to yearn for nothing more than to participate in God's love for eternity—this person speaks out of this love of God, and together with him the entire church-community of Jesus Christ: We have peace with God. We boast in our afflictions. The love of God is poured out into our heart. Amen. (476)

Community life also continued many familiar practices despite the change in venue. In a letter dated February 2, 1939, Gerhard Lehne, a student in the sixth group, describes his experience. He admits that he was not anxious to come to Gross Schlönwitz, in part because he was a free-spirited person who loved the outdoors and did not relish joining a community of fellow theologians, and in part because an acquaintance had felt constricted at Finkenwalde (127–28). But things went much better than he had feared. He writes that at the seminary

> I entered a world that united many things that I love and need: accurate theological work on the ground of fellowship . . . true

fellowship under the Word that united all "without respect to person" . . . and love for everything that makes even this fallen creation still worthy of love: music, sports, and the beauty of the earth; a generous style of life that favorably combined the culture of old homes with the uninhibited forms of a community of young men—last, not least, a man in charge whom one can indeed admire without reservation. (128)

He follows this description with another that gives a vivid picture of the community having afternoon tea while discussing theological issues and news (128). That his portrait includes a reference to Bonhoeffer's frequent absences indicates the extensive nature of the director's activities and the help he received from Bethge and Onnasch.

In late April 1938 the seventh group of Bonhoeffer's seminarians began their studies. The term concluded at the end of August. As will be discussed below, this session and the next unfolded against the backdrop of two major controversies, a fact that made life no easier for the students or for Bonhoeffer and his colleagues. Besides the normal teaching and pastoral duties, Bonhoeffer lectured on the Pastoral Epistles (322–43). He was doing his best to integrate his theology of the church and his theology of pastoral ministry through his commitment to following God's Word.

The eighth session began October 17–19, just days after Bonhoeffer completed writing *Life Together*, and ended March 8, 1939. A student from this session, Hans-Werner Jensen, later recounted, "I had the great pleasure of typing the manuscript [of *Life Together*] to his dictation."[3] Jensen's recollections of his time in Gross Schlönwitz demonstrate that life together continued. He observes that

Bonhoeffer wanted a genuine, natural community in the Preachers' Seminary, and this community was practiced in play, in walks through the richly wooded and beautiful district of Pomerania, during evenings spent in listening to someone

---

[3] Wolf-Dieter Zimmermann and Ronald Gregor Smith, eds., *I Knew Dietrich Bonhoeffer*, trans. Kathe Gregor Smith (New York: Harper and Row, 1966), 152.

reading . . . in making music and singing, and last not least in worship together and holy communion.[4]

During this term Bonhoeffer and his students studied key New Testament concepts related to spiritual life and ministerial practice, as they had done in Finkenwalde.[5] Using the general methodology found in Kittel's famous wordbook, they examined sin, temptation, patience/endurance, testing/probation, joy, peace, abstinence/self-control, death, and gratitude (344–82). This approach forced the students and Bonhoeffer to examine a wide range of Old and New Testament texts, and was an excellent assignment for students doing research in their professor's absence.

Controversies

Clearly, there was sufficient work to be done at the seminary sites alone. But there was more than this to tire Bonhoeffer, his students, and his colleagues. Controversy is especially wearying to all people except those with combative personalities. Pressure exerted on a person and his or her cause by external forces is wearing. Yet few things can exhaust an individual like a controversy fueled by disagreement within that person's own circles. This type of dispute tempts one to wonder if a given cause has been worth all the sacrifices one has made, or if the cause will survive in any case. Bonhoeffer faced at least two such controversies in 1938–1939.

THE OATH-TO-HITLER CONTROVERSY

The first controversy involved the Confessing Church in what Bethge denounces as "its most shameful affair."[6] In April 1938, just before the summer term began, the official head of Lutheran churches ordered all pastors to take an oath of loyalty to Hitler in honor of Germany's annexation of Austria. Failure to do so would result in termination. Bonhoeffer was not required to comply, given the

---

[4] Ibid., 155.
[5] See *DBW* 14:476–87.
[6] Bethge, *DB*, 599.

position he held, but he opposed the oath for obvious reasons. How could some within the Confessing Church stand against the Aryan clause, among other things, and yet take this oath? One reason was that pastors in Confessing Churches who still retained government support, even though they embraced the Barmen Declaration and Dahlem decisions,[7] stood to lose their incomes. Another was that young theologians hoping to be called to a pastorate would forfeit such possibilities. Yet another was that some considered taking the oath a mere formality.

The Confessing Church synod of June 11–13 debated the matter, and on July 31, 1938, the church officials allowed pastors to take the oath, which in any case a majority had already done.[8] Bonhoeffer wrote a stern letter of disagreement to his superiors dated August 11, 1938.[9] In August the government informed the churches that the oath was not necessary. Hitler had not insisted on it; the church leader had ordered it on his own.[10] The whole humiliating business had been as unnecessary as it was debilitating in the end. But at least it had come to an end.

THE LEGALIZATION CONTROVERSY

The second controversy lasted longer. Indeed, it remained an issue well into the war years.[11] This controversy revolved around pressures on seminarians and former seminarians to become "legalized" ministers, in short, ministers in good standing with the dominant church and state governments.[12] As was noted in previous chapters, one of Bonhoeffer's students took this route as early as 1935. So this discussion was not just a theoretical one to Bonhoeffer. He had staked his life's work on the connection between Barmen (confession of truth) and Dahlem (separation from a heretical church),

---

[7] On this point, see Schlingensiepen, *DB*, 212.
[8] Bethge, *DB*, 601.
[9] See *DBW* 15:52–58.
[10] Bethge, *DB*, 601.
[11] See *DBW* 16:265.
[12] See Victoria Barnett, *For the Soul of the People: Protestant Protest against Hitler* (New York: Oxford University Press, 1992), 94–98, for a more detailed discussion of the issues surrounding this controversy.

and he was preparing young theologians to do the same. Returning to this matter over and over again tired all concerned, including Bonhoeffer.

But he was willing to return to it again and again nonetheless. During June 20–25, 1938, some forty-five of his former students gathered at Zingst for a retreat.[13] Schlingensiepen writes that the event took place "when the Confessing Church was truly at its lowest ebb, and Bonhoeffer made passionate efforts to ensure that his former students remained loyal to it."[14] The retreat featured discussions of common pastoral interest, such as evangelizing, conducting confirmation classes, and preaching.[15] Enduring in current churches, finding a place to serve, and legalization were also discussed.[16] Bonhoeffer spoke personally with many of the young pastors about legalization. He also offered searching and stimulating lectures on the sixth petition of the Lord's Prayer ("lead us not into temptation") and on the temptation of Christ and the relationship of these passages to the situation they all faced.[17] Though Bonhoeffer clearly wished his former students to stand firm on the matter of legalization, at this meeting he and the others agreed to extend love and ministry to former students who had decided to become legalized.[18]

The lectures on temptation Bonhoeffer gave at Zingst have been published in more than one format, including together with Bonhoeffer's 1933 volume *Creation and Fall* in an English edition in 1968, the format in which I first read both works. The pairing was effective for considering a biblical theology of creation, fall, and redemption, but it did not offer a particularly good sense of the material's original context. The lectures are penetrating in any case, but having even a limited grasp of the historical context makes them even more so.

Bonhoeffer returned to the subject of perseverance in a circular

---

[13] Bethge, *DB*, 593.
[14] Schlingensiepen, *DB*, 212.
[15] See *DBW* 15:49–52.
[16] Ibid., 15:50.
[17] For the text of the lectures, consult *DBW* 15:386–415.
[18] See Bethge, *DB*, 593; and *DBW* 15:47–52.

letter to former students dated August 23, 1938. In it he offers a meditation on Colossians 2:8 and exhorts them, "Do not let anyone divert you from your goal." He encourages his readers by declaring, "The victory prize is sure to be yours as long as you don't let yourselves be misled in the decisive moment and reach for other means and ways to reach the goal" (60). He then sets forth three directives he believes come from the text. First, they should not seek an individual solution to the problem. They will "win the victory in the fellowship of our brethren or not at all" (60). Second, they should not listen to those who "press us to find a solution for all difficulties at all costs. . . . They make us forget that our goal is not to be comfortable and free of conflict but to win the victory prize after a completed run" (60). Third, they must not listen to those who tell them they have suffered enough and it is time to make peace with the government, for there is nothing to expect from the government. He warns, "The false reliance on works that depends on the church's so-called state is just as godless as any other and must deprive us of the victory prize" (60–61). In short, he believes perseverance will be vindicated. Near the end of the letter he conveys the news that two former students had recently taken steps to be legalized (61).

These strong words to his former students do not tell the whole story. He writes of his own weariness and desire to persevere in his work in a personal letter to Erwin Sutz dated September 18, 1938. In general Bonhoeffer wrote as freely and openly to Sutz as he did to anyone. He tells his old friend from Union Seminary days:

> I long greatly for a few quiet months for scholarly work. . . .
> In remotest eastern Pomerania, one rather loses contact with
> the world. There is simply too much to do, too, that no time
> remains for quiet correspondence. One needs the little spare
> time that remains for one's own work. But the work continues
> to bring pleasure while continuing to grow. (72)

He adds that though each day is a gift, when one forgets this simple truth, it is easy to want to choose "a somewhat more settled

existence, with all the 'rights' that one otherwise has at this . . .
age" (72). Yet to make this choice "would mean the abandonment
of the work," something he cannot do (72). He is determined to set
aside his personal weariness for the sake of persevering in the work
before him, but clearly he feels strained.

On October 26, 1938, again just days after finishing *Life Together* and beginning a new term, Bonhoeffer delivered a searing
lecture, "The Path of the Young Illegal Theologians of the Confessing Church." The occasion was a special meeting of the Confessing
Church in Pomerania called to discuss the legalization issue because
national church leaders had set a deadline for the nonlegalized pastors to come into line.[19] Bethge notes that the situation was grim.
In the past, 318 of 600 Pomeranian clergy had committed to the
Confessing Church, but now only 60 of these had not sought legalization. Furthermore, there were 57 young illegal theologians, of
which 17 had regular pastorates, 22 were in nonsanctioned positions, and the rest had no positions at all. And the churches were
only raising half the money needed to support the illegals.[20] Bonhoeffer had been asked to speak to the group. His comments were
reproduced and sent to the young theologians in Pomerania (416).

In his lecture he questions why the church keeps returning to the
issue of legalization (416–18). Have its members lost faith in God's
direction at Barmen and Dahlem? Do they desire stability and peace
so much that they will accept heresy? To deal appropriately with
these matters they must turn to the Bible (419). An examination
of the Bible indicates that "Scriptural evidence applies only to the
truth of a doctrine, but never to the correctness of a path" (419). In
other words, Scripture does not cover every possible step on a path.
One walks the path only by faith as one follows the truth (419).
Bonhoeffer asserts that the Bible does not concern itself with our
individual desire to know or have a particular path in life, especially a comfortable one. The truth must therefore be our primary

---

[19] Bethge, *DB*, 611–13.
[20] Ibid., 613.

concern, for if "we abide in truth and in truth alone, our path will be the right one" (420).

An examination of the Bible also shows that the Scriptures do not reveal every detail of any particular course of action (420). Rather, the Bible requires one to follow Christ in faith as a doer of truth. Bonhoeffer notes that some of his Confessing Church colleagues asked for clear biblical evidence that they were on the right path to refuse to become legalized. To them he replies that the Bible does not fulfill their request for certainty, "because it [the Bible] is not intended to be an insurance policy for our paths, which may become dangerous. The Bible does only one thing: it calls us to faith and obedience in the truth that we know in Jesus Christ. Scripture points not to our paths but to the truth of God" (420).

Moreover, the Bible teaches that those who want full assurance concerning every step do not wish to live in faith (421). Those who wish to retain the Barmen Confession and deny Dahlem's decisions forget that a confession must take concrete form. It must choose a path. A confession without a form cannot be the body of Christ (422). Bonhoeffer once again declares his commitment to a visible church, writing, "Church is not a community of souls, as is claimed today, nor is church merely the proclamation of the gospel; that is to say, church is not only the pulpit, but church is the real body of Christ on earth" (422). He continues, "Just as Jesus Christ was not a truth or an idea but flesh, that is to say, a human being in the body, likewise the church is the earthly body of the heavenly head" (422). Christ is the Head of the church, and the body must follow the Head's will (422).

To be more specific, "The church is essentially an assembly around the word and sacrament, but in addition it is the fullness of the gifts, offices, and powers that are effective within the church community" (422). Therefore, "Ultimately, the church means the life of the church-community according to the commandments of God. The church is thus the space of proclamation, the space of order, the space of Christian life. It is all these things as the body of Christ" (422). To let go of the proper order of the church (Dahlem) anchored in truth as opposed to heresy (Barmen), then, would be to dismember the body. Again, there is no such thing as an invisible body.

The main part of the lecture then makes six assertions. Bonhoeffer claims that the church is a unity; the church needs leadership; the church's leadership serves the proclamation of the gospel and the discipline of the church; the church's proclamation is tied to its commission from Christ; obedience to a heretical church is disobedience to Christ; and the church leaves all matters of concern related to the future in God's hands (423–24). Though each point is vital to Bonhoeffer's argument, several of the first five points have been examined at least briefly in previous chapters. The sixth point has tremendous importance for this juncture of Bonhoeffer's life.

In his discussion of this point Bonhoeffer reminds his audience that one can never know what the future holds. Therefore, he claims, "We will only become free of worry when we abide firmly in the truth that we know and let ourselves be guided by it alone. But if we stare at the waves rather than looking to the Lord, then we will be lost" (434). He feels that too many of his brothers are pointing to the waves as evidence that they are on the wrong path. Furthermore, he thinks God has already spoken to them through the actions he led them to take at Barmen, Dahlem, and beyond (435). Going back on those decisions, in his opinion, is really a rejection of "God's grace and call" (435). It is also a desertion of the young theologians who followed Dahlem (435–36). These men committed themselves to the Confessing Church when that meant no prospects for the future. Meanwhile, some pastors could affirm Dahlem in the safety of their churches, since they did not give up their salaries. The real test has come for them now.

Bonhoeffer closes by calling for faithfulness to the path they have begun (436–37). As he does so his general weariness and his passion for his cause are both evident. He thinks the Confessing Church has spent the last few years constantly revisiting legalization, and he believes this situation "has gradually become an unbearable burden for those who would like to move on" (436). The path they are already on is the path of truth, the path of freedom, the path of integrity, and the path of godly endurance. Only this path can lead to God's guidance and to joy (437). He closes with a very personal reference: "When I took on this lecture, I asked a brother—who today finds himself in the difficult position of making a decision—what I should say. He answered: 'Take up your cross and follow me.' I think that this brother was correct" (437).

In a letter to former students dated November 20, 1938, Bonhoeffer returns to the subject of endurance on the right path. He greets them with a quotation of Romans 15:5, in which Paul prays, "May the God of endurance and encouragement grant you to live in such harmony with one another, in accord with Jesus Christ" (82). He notes that he and his current students are studying "the New Testament concept of patient endurance" (see above) and reports that he has come to the conclusion that "in essence the only issue at stake is whether we are willing to learn from the gospel what patient endurance means" (82). Currently, he observes, the Confessing Church continues to ask if they are going down the right path, given all they have suffered. But to him this is the wrong approach, for Paul and Luther found joy in the midst of their afflictions, not only in the absence of them (82). Those who "take part in the patient endurance of Jesus" will become patient (83). Those who become impatient on the path due to affliction and trouble will divide the body, for impatience always divides (83). Those who remain on the path of faith and patience will endure, and God will enable them to help one another in hard times (83).

Bonhoeffer's letters that date from December 1938 to February 1939 demonstrate the ebb and flow of the legalization controversy. They also reflect the wear and tear of ministry he now felt. On the one hand, he received letters from former students that must have encouraged him. Two students from the third session wrote agreeing with the need for patience and courage (96–97). A student from the fourth group wrote, "In no way may Christ for us become a means to an end" (87). Another from the same group wrote to tell his former teacher how grateful he was that God had protected Bonhoeffer so he could train more seminarians (132–34). From a student in the fifth group came a letter telling Bonhoeffer how much *The Cost of Discipleship* had meant to him. He hoped this greeting would encourage Bonhoeffer in light of two other former students' decisions to become legalized (120–22). The writer says: "It was so urgent for me to write this letter to you; perhaps you will gather from this that your work in Finkenwalde has not been for nothing. I could imagine that because of the events in Pomerania your spirits are low" (121). The very heartening letter from Gerhard Lehne, the student from the sixth session cited above, came during this time as well (127–30). One also arrived from a seventh-session student who had taken steps to be legalized. In it the writer stated that he had received Bonhoeffer's October 26 lecture and was going to reverse his decision (135).

On the other hand, he received letters bearing unwelcome news and wrote letters describing his tiredness. One of the students who had decided to become legalized wrote a respectful letter of substantial disagreement with Bonhoeffer (148–51). In a letter to Wilhelm Rott, his colleague at Finkenwalde (who had since suffered imprisonment), Bonhoeffer wrote that he was not certain how long the seminary ministry could continue (124). To his brother Karl-Friedrich he confided in a letter dated January 28, 1939, "It has been at times very depressing in the last few weeks, when one must see how many people are seeking quiet and security at all costs and using all kinds of pretexts and reasons" (115). He notes that these depressing things had come alongside the normal heavy work of lectures and other labors (115). But he rallies, asserting, "It is entirely certain to me that for the church it all depends upon whether we now hold on, even with great sacrifices. . . . I wouldn't know anything worth a full commitment today if not this" (115). Despite his determination, however, he states that he hopes to take some time away to visit his twin sister, Sabine, and her family in March, if possible (116). This visit came at a crucial juncture of Bonhoeffer's own journey on the path of patient endurance.

By February 14, 1939, Bonhoeffer reflected on what he considered very good news in a letter to his former students. At a synod at the end of January the Confessing Church had taken a position against legalization (144). For the moment at least, the issue was put to rest. Bonhoeffer thanks the letter's recipients for their encouraging response to his November 20, 1938, letter. He then observes that in that previous letter he focused on the concept of endurance, one he and the current students had been analyzing. Given the recent synod, he now brings their attention to another concept the group had studied, the concept of joy (144). Bonhoeffer admits that the new situation "liberated us from a dull pressure" and restored "the full joy of Christ" (144). Taking joy in Christ reminds Bonhoeffer, "Whoever has found Jesus Christ goes along Christ's path with joy, goes there with joy, and sells everything he possesses and purchases the precious pearl (Matt. 13:44)" (145).

But the reverse is also true: "Whoever does not follow the path of Jesus will become sad like the rich young man (Matt. 19:22)" (145). Such joy will occur even in the midst of much suffering, which Bonhoeffer knew had to be the case with many of his former students (145). Pressures from within and without were still daily realities. Yet as believers embrace the path of joy, the church becomes a community of joy recognizing that the "origin of all true joy is God's joy in us" (146). This is one of the most upbeat letters Bonhoeffer ever wrote to his former students. Yet subsequent events would test his commitment to suffering with joy and his faithfulness to the path of Christ's calling.

The Path of Faithfulness: 1939–1940

The eighth term ended March 8, 1939. Bonhoeffer and Bethge traveled to England to see Bonhoeffer's sister and her family, as Bonhoeffer had planned. They arrived there March 12 and Bonhoeffer extended his stay until April 18, 1939. Much occurred in the interim. On March 15–16 Germany invaded Czechoslovakia. On April 4 the German Christians declared their desire for the national church to be completely free of Jews. While in England Bonhoeffer met with several ecumenical and academic contacts, and he spoke to expatriate German pastors, the group of which he had once been a part.[21] Bethge notes that Bonhoeffer stayed longer than expected in England, perhaps hoping war would break out and leave him stuck there.[22]

Germany's war preparations now pressed upon Bonhoeffer and his friends in the Confessing Church, and indeed upon every man in their age groups, as military conscription gathered pace. Most of the Confessing Church pastors were willing to serve in the military, though Bonhoeffer was not. His birth year was called to report to the authorities as early as November 1938, but he later faced a deadline of May 22, 1939, to report to the military for assignment or declare himself a conscientious objector and face trial. Others who took this latter route had been shot.[23]

One other option was open, and Bonhoeffer pursued it. He applied for a year's extension for the purpose of studying in the United States, and his request was granted.[24] It must be noted that the Confessing Church leadership wanted Bonhoeffer to take this step to save him from likely harm and to save the Confessing Church from likely repercussions related to his refusal to serve as a soldier.[25] That he was in grave danger was certainly the understanding of people trying to help Bonhoeffer from England and the United States.[26]

Bonhoeffer wrote his former students again at the end of May 1939 (166). The tone of the letter is very cheerful. He notes that since his last letter on February 14 much has happened. Though

---

[21] Ibid., 635–41.
[22] Ibid., 648.
[23] Ibid., 635.
[24] Ibid.
[25] Note Hellmut Traub's recollections in Zimmermann and Smith, *I Knew Dietrich Bonhoeffer*, 156–61.
[26] See, for example, the letter from Reinhold Niebuhr to Henry Smith Leiper dated May 1, 1939, in *DBW* 15:161–62.

some have abandoned the cause, others have been heartened and are standing strong (166). The wearing effects of further controversy have thereby been avoided, and prospects for the future now look bright (167). Then at the end of the brief letter he abruptly states: "Our work goes on. I will now travel for several months to the seminary where I formerly studied for one year. After that I will return to this same work. But Eberhard and Fritz will take care of . . . all that is most necessary" (167). With these few words the former students he had urged to stay the course learned he would be going to a much safer place with war looming. Though most knew of Bonhoeffer's views on taking up arms, one has to believe that not all receiving this news would have understood his reasons for going, nor would they have agreed if they did.

It is not my purpose to recount and debate all the possible reasons why Bonhoeffer left Germany so swiftly and came back just as suddenly. There are several good studies of these matters in the literature on Bonhoeffer. I simply wish to note a few clear stages in his thought process and stress that getting back on the path he had been urging others to follow became the unmistakable will of God for his life as far as he was concerned. And getting back on the path meant getting back to his seminary work, which any fair reading of his letters and diaries from this time indicate he missed very much.

From the moment he departed Berlin for the United States on June 2, 1939, Bonhoeffer was haunted by thoughts of the seminarians and colleagues who remained behind. Even before leaving Berlin he was bothered that no successor had been named director of the seminary.[27] He left a simple and touching set of instructions for whoever that person would be in a letter dated May 28, 1939. He called his position "one of the most gratifying tasks in the CC" (171). He wrote that his replacement would find "two coworkers who have stood in this work for over four years and who have borne full responsibility for the leadership of the houses for one and a half years, to whom therefore the leadership of the communal life

---

[27] Bethge, *DB*, 649.

can be entrusted, whenever he himself is not able to be there" (171). He explained what the students had been doing and what they should study next, and he advised the successor "to take walks or otherwise spend as much time as possible together with the brothers" (172). Eventually Hellmut Traub, a former student of Barth's, was named to the post.

The journey to the United States included a stop in England for a brief visit with his sister and her family. Bonhoeffer arrived in New York on June 12, 1939. Very shortly he became aware that British and American friends had concluded that, given his views on military service, Bonhoeffer could not return to Germany at the end of his year's leave. They assumed he faced a concentration camp or worse. Thus, he was offered a post working as a pastor to German refugees in New York.[28] The friends were also pursuing other opportunities for him.[29] It therefore came as a surprise to them when on June 20 he stated that he had taken a year's leave from his Confessing Church work and could not accept the refugee ministry, since he believed doing so would preclude a return to Germany. The year's leave postponed the decision regarding military service; it did not allow him to immigrate. He would have to deal with the military issue as events unfolded.[30] Of course, what he told his would-be protectors was basically in keeping with what he related to his former students in his May 14 letter.

Soon Bonhoeffer decided not to stay the year. In fact, he left for Germany on July 7–8, again stopping through England. He arrived in Berlin July 30, and he was back with the seminarians for a retreat by August 4–14. Thus, he was with the students and his colleagues, now living in Köslin and Sigurdshof, when the ninth term ended on August 24–25, 1939.

---

[28] See, for example, the related correspondence between Reinhold Niebuhr and Henry Smith Leiper in *DBW* 15:161–62, 169; the letter from Bonhoeffer to Henry Smith Leiper in *DBW* 15:182–85; and the letter from Henry Smith Leiper to Samuel McCrea Cavert in *DBW* 15:185–86.
[29] See, for instance, the letter from Paul Lehmann to Bonhoeffer in *DBW* 15:170–71; the letter from John Baillie to Bonhoeffer in *DBW* 15:186; and the letter from Paul Lehmann to colleges and seminaries seeking speaking opportunities for Bonhoeffer in *DBW* 15:201–3.
[30] Note the letters from Bonhoeffer to Henry Smith Leiper in *DBW* 15:182–85; and from Bonhoeffer to Paul Lehmann in *DBW* 15:191–92.

Without question, there were many reasons why Bonhoeffer reversed his decision to be away for a year as abruptly as he had made it. Again, there are good analyses of his decision-making process in other works. Given the purpose of this book I will focus on only one reason, his love for the seminary work and his desire to return to it. On June 11, 1939, with no worship service to attend, and thinking of his German brothers having their service, he writes in his diary, "If only the doubts about my own path were overcome" (219). On June 15, as he considers his ease in America, at this point only a few days old, he writes, "This inactivity, or rather activity spent on trivialities, is simply no longer bearable for us, thinking of the brothers and the precious time" (222). The next day he admits, "Only fourteen days ago today from Berlin, and already so filled with longing for the work again" (223). The day after declaring his decision not to take up the refugee post, he writes that "the joy in the work at home" looms large in his thinking (228).

Similarly, he writes on June 24 that he "must get back to the work" (230). On June 26, having read 2 Timothy 4:21, in which Paul asks Timothy to "come before winter," Bonhoeffer observes:

> That is haunting me the whole day. We seem to feel like the soldiers on leave from the front who, despite all that awaits them, push to return to the front. We can't come free of it. Not as if we were necessary, as if we were needed (by God!?), but simply because our life is there and because we desert our life, annihilate it, if we are not part of things there. (232)

In the end, Bonhoeffer could not reconcile the path he had taken and the path of faithfulness to God's call in his life. He did not know where the path would end, but he knew the next step required going home.

By July 11, Bethge had news that Bonhoeffer was returning. In a letter to Bonhoeffer that day he relates:

> Yes, Dietrich—your return. When I announced it, it naturally provoked an outburst of enthusiasm, and there is the energetic

wish to have the offer [Bonhoeffer's offer to return to his post] come true and herewith I pass it on. The only one whom this filled with ambivalent feelings is Potsdam [Bethge's nickname for Hellmut Traub, Bonhoeffer's successor], who simply likes it here very well. (246)

In his recollections of events, Traub gives other reasons than liking his new post for his ambivalence over Bonhoeffer's homecoming. He mentions being relieved when Bonhoeffer had gotten out of Germany, for he thought Bonhoeffer would be a key player in the renewal of church life in Germany once the impending war ended:

I was happy to know that Bonhoeffer was not in Germany, but safe from the coming reign of terror, and the catastrophe which I was convinced would follow. He must not perish in it. . . . He was practically predestined to rebuild the Protestant church after the debacle which most certainly was in store for us. (A rebuilding which we imagined differently, however). . . . Over and above this, and apart from the great danger of his situation, Bonhoeffer was sure to find no mercy, as he was bound to be a conscientious objector.[31]

Traub may have had different views than Bonhoeffer on a variety of subjects, but he clearly had deep respect for him.

Much to Traub's surprise and consternation, "then one day, after a short message that he was returning, Bonhoeffer stood before us."[32] Traub recalls that he asked Bonhoeffer why he had returned "after it had cost so much trouble to get him to safety—safety for us, for our cause; here everything was lost anyway."[33] Traub had thought that few faithful members of the Confessing Church would survive the war.

According to Traub, in response Bonhoeffer

calmly lit a cigarette. Then he said he had made a mistake in going to America. . . . He gave us two reasons for his return.

---

[31] Zimmermann and Smith, *I Knew Dietrich Bonhoeffer*, 158–59.
[32] Ibid., 159.
[33] Ibid.

First, simply his thought of the Confessing Church, which meant for him all the many young brethren, had not given him any rest. He could not stay away from them, he must not leave them. This meant—and this was the second reason—that he could not watch Germany's fate from outside and have no part in it.[34]

As far as Bonhoeffer was concerned, the faithful path back to Köslin and Sigurdshof was necessary. He could not be invisible. His witness as part of the body of Christ required a concrete, on-the-ground presence among those he loved. He had to be part of the living body of Christ, and that meant being at the seminary again when the term concluded in late August.

The Path of Faithfulness: *Meditations on Psalm 119*

Germany invaded Poland on September 1, 1939, which finally led England and France to declare the war Bonhoeffer had long expected. Though Germany gained a swift victory, it was not without cost to Hitler's armies. In particular, Bonhoeffer's first student to be imprisoned also became the first killed in battle.[35] Bonhoeffer reports this loss in a letter to former students dated September 20, 1939 (273). Dozens more former students eventually followed in this colleague's footsteps. At the end of the letter Bonhoeffer also reports, "I have been back from my journey for several weeks. The day before yesterday was Fritz's wedding" (277). The Fritz he mentions is Onnasch, who had labored with Bonhoeffer and Bethge at Köslin and Gross Schlönwitz. As in the past, Bonhoeffer went forward with the seminary ministry in the midst of uncertainty and death, yet also among signs that life's joys cannot be extinguished.

At the end of October Bonhoeffer and Bethge began the tenth and final term of their seminary work together. Few ministerial candidates remained in the Confessing Church or in any other church. Victoria Barnett writes, "The war quickly cut the ranks of theological students and young pastors. There were around 2,000

---

[34] Ibid., 159–60.
[35] Schlingensiepen, *DB*, 234.

theological students in the last prewar semester in 1939; by February 1940, there were 38."[36] Eight students joined Bonhoeffer and Bethge at Sigurdshof (see chapter 2). There were not enough candidates to need the Köslin site, and Sigurdshof's isolation made it the safer place. Bethge describes the eight as coming

> from Berlin, Pomerania, Westphalia, and the Rhineland. They began their work with Bonhoeffer in primitive conditions, and relied on their own ingenuity to solve the problems of obtaining coal, paraffin, petrol, and food. They succeeded, both threatened and protected by one of the most severe winters. Only one ordinand was taken away from the course by the recruiting officials.[37]

Community life and pastoral preparation continued in what all must have thought would be the final session for some time.

There seems to have been no panic in Bonhoeffer as he undertook his teaching, unlike the outlook evident in some of his letters during the spring. As winter set in, he wrote to former students again during Advent, mourning the loss of yet another of their number who had died in military service, assuring them he was praying for them, requesting their prayers in return, and letting them know, "On a limited scale our work proceeds as before" (288–90). He received birthday greetings, including one from Fritz Onnasch, who wrote, "May God gently guide you along his path through your new year of life, continue to transform your gifts into the ministry to his church and the brothers who are being placed on your way . . ." (294). Bonhoeffer taught as before and wrote on Psalm 119, a passage that helped him collect his thoughts on the joyous Christian path, patient endurance in calling, and the primacy of God's Word. In short, he looked at discipleship from angles old and new to understand better the path he walked with God.

Bonhoeffer had long been interested in Psalm 119.[38] The relative

---

[36] Barnett, *For the Soul of the People*, 96.
[37] Bethge, *DB*, 666.
[38] See Bethge's brief description of this interest in *DB*, 667, and the excellent introduction to Bonhoeffer's engagement with Psalms in Dietrich Bonhoeffer, *Meditating on the Word*, trans. and ed.

solitude at Sigurdshof now gave him the impetus to commit some of his thoughts on this magnificent psalm to paper. Psalm 119 is a special version of a Hebrew acrostic poem, one that utilizes the order of the Hebrew alphabet. The psalm begins with eight verses, each of which starts with the first letter of the alphabet; the psalm then proceeds to a second group of eight verses, each of which begins with the second Hebrew letter, and so forth. There are twenty-two letters in the Hebrew alphabet and thus 176 verses in the psalm.

Psalm 119 exhibits great artistry, slow movement within and between each set of eight verses, and much enriching overlap within its thematic development. In this way it is more like a long musical piece than a linear argument. Bonhoeffer shows facility in navigating these artistic and theological waters. He prepared a sentence outline and a topical outline for the whole chapter that shows what he attempted in his comments on verses 1–21 and gives glimpses of what he hoped to accomplish in the whole work. The sentence outlines indicate that he thought 119:1–8 consists of "Praise of the walking in the law," 119:9–16 emphasizes "The blameless way," and 119:17–24 highlights "Illumination—wonder of the eyes opened by law" (527). Thus, his outline and succeeding comments indicate his ongoing interest in three great themes: walking in God's path, the relationship of the law and Christian discipleship, and the importance of seeking the illumination of God's Word.

Bonhoeffer reflects on the first two of these themes in his analysis of 119:1. As was discussed earlier in this chapter, for some time he had been frustrated by the Confessing Church's constant reexamination of fundamental truths and the church's path. He had also struggled with understanding his own path during his time in New York. So with more than a hint of gratitude, he writes concerning verse 1: "Whoever speaks this way presumes that the beginning has already occurred. He points out that the life with God consists not only and not essentially of ever-new beginnings. Therefore, the

---

David Gracie (New York: Ballantine, 1986), 1–20. Purchasing this latter volume when it appeared gave me my first opportunity to read Bonhoeffer's comments on Psalm 119, and I remain very grateful for Gracie's work.

psalmist calls it a change, a walking in God's law" (496). This means that since "God's beginning with us has already occurred, our life with God is a path being walked within God's law" (497). This walking in God's law is not based on fear and should not result in unhappy servitude. "No, it is the freedom from the murderous law of never-ending beginnings" (497). Having to go back endlessly to the beginning in one's path with God "is the complete destruction of faith in that God who set the beginning once through his forgiving and renewing word in Jesus Christ, that is, in my baptism, in my rebirth, in my conversion" (497). As in *The Cost of Discipleship*, Bonhoeffer links justification and sanctification in his description of the whole Christian life.

Having received God's new beginning once and for all, the believer and the community of faith walk in the law as a joyful path taken with God and one another. Their path settled by God's beginning, Christians walk "within God's law" (497). This means their life, their walk, "is the life under the word of God in its utter multitude of forms, in its richness, in its inexhaustible fullness of knowledge and experiences" (497), not in the sense of being under its condemnation. Thus, this walking is never dull, lifeless, or lacking in possibilities. To explain further, he comments, "Whoever is caught in the search for a new beginning is *under* the law and is worn down and killed by it. Whoever comes from the found beginning is *within* the law of God, is upheld and preserved by it for life" (498). Having found the beginning he needs and the path he must walk, the psalmist finds joy in walking within the law of God, who has given him all he needs to live.

Next, Bonhoeffer discusses the nature of God's law and its role in believers' lives. One must grasp that God's redemption and God's law go together, though one must also understand that redemption precedes law. The law proceeds inextricably with "God's act of redemption" and "God's promise" (498). Joined by God, these must not be separated. God gave the law to Moses only after redeeming Israel from Egypt, and only then after promising to do so

(498–99). Since this is true, thinking through the Bible as a whole, "whoever asks about the law will be reminded of Jesus Christ and the redemption from servitude in sin and death that in him has been accomplished for all human beings and will be reminded of the new beginning set by God in Jesus Christ for all human beings" (499).

As in *The Cost of Discipleship* and *Life Together*, Bonhoeffer treats the Bible as a whole linked by Jesus Christ. He refuses to dichotomize the Testaments by dividing law from grace. As a result, he claims, "God's law is inseparable from his redemptive deed. . . . God gives his law to those whom he loves, whom God has chosen and accepted (Deut. 7:7–11). To know God's law is grace and joy (Deut. 4:6–10). It is the way of life for those who accept the grace of God (Lev. 18:5)" (499).

Connecting God's redemptive promises and God's commanded way of life leads one to understand how the psalmist can call those who walk in God's ways blessed, or "happy" (500). This happiness is physical as well as spiritual. It includes the believer's well-being (500). Bonhoeffer comments that some Christians focus only on spiritual well-being and consider God's gifts of physical well-being a relic of Old Testament belief (501). In a tone that seems part scornful and part playful, Bonhoeffer states that such people "want to be more spiritual than God," who gave us the Bible (500). These people "want to be schoolmasters of the Holy Scripture and thus deny themselves the full joy of their Christianity and deny God the thanksgiving that is owed to his great kindness" (501). Bonhoeffer's spirituality was always a very disciplined one. But it was also quite life affirming, quite appreciative of nature, art, music, and other forms of beauty. Such joys *flow from* walking in God's law; they do not exist *despite* God's law.

This happiness exists in the midst of difficulty, sorrow, and loss. As he had done several times before in his writings of 1937–1939, Bonhoeffer explains that trouble does not negate joy. Believers know life is not perfect, but they know everything they receive comes from God's hand (502). "They know that the good gifts of creation are there for their sake so that they confess Christ in praise and thankfulness and proclaim him as the Lord of the world" (502). They also learn firsthand the truth of Jesus's promise that those who leave family and lands will receive brothers and sisters in Christ and the kingdom of God (502). They learn that suffering is not outside God's realm. Bonhoeffer observes, perhaps with his deceased students in mind,

> But if God should indeed give the cup of suffering for Christ's sake to one of his own to drink, to the bitter end of the cross and death, with which God has honored only a few throughout the ages, he will have certainly prepared their hearts in such a way that it will be these who will witness with a strong faith in a new and powerful way: "Happy are those who walk in the law of the Lord." (502)

They learn all these things not just as individuals, but also together within the community of faith (502).

With this strong introduction in place, Bonhoeffer continues to emphasize God's path, God's law, and God's gift of happiness in his comments on Psalm 119:2–8. Verse 2 stresses the heart as the key to walking with God. God's law reminds believers that he is the Lord of all parts of life; so, "Not only lips and hands but the entire undivided heart must be involved. It must search continuously for the one of whom the testimonies speak" (503). As one seeks God with the heart, one walks continuously along the path blazed by God, according to verse 3 (504). Thankfully, "God knows the entire way; we only know the next step and the final goal. There is no standing still; every day, every hour, one progresses" (504).

Bonhoeffer next notes that the "entire gospel message of salvation" is often called "the way" in the New Testament, which is in keeping with Psalm 119 (504). Since the Christian life is a way, not merely a concept, "the gospel and faith are not a timeless idea but an action of God and of the human being in history" (504). The path is real because it is God's path (505). It is real because God encounters us as we walk this path (505; see v. 4), because we learn that we cannot be pious on our own (506; see v. 5), because we discover that we cannot count on our power or reputation (507; see v. 6), and because life is diverse and colorful and rich (507–8; see v. 6). It is real because we have to "renounce our pious egos so that God can do his work with us" (509; see v. 8). Then we can truly wish to keep God's statutes (v. 8), not because we "are compelled to do it," but because God has freed us to want what we used to hate (510).

When these concrete lessons are learned, we will understand that misfortunes and trials are not the worst things that can happen to us. The worst thing that can happen is to feel that God is not with us (510), since we understand daily that God's grace makes walking in his law possible. As Bonhoeffer summarizes the section: "Thus the circle is completed. God's grace stood at the beginning; it makes our beginning so that we may be freed from our own beginnings. Grace puts us on the way, and it is grace that we call upon, step-by-step" (511).

Praise for the law and the path it gives the believer in Psalm 119:1–8 leads to desiring to understand how one may be blameless in this path in 119:9–16. Examining the nature of the blameless way gives Bonhoeffer the opportunity to stress another of his favorite themes, the truth and power of God's Word. In verse 9, a young man asks how to keep his way "blameless," knowing full well that his sins teach him he is powerless to be blameless in his own strength (511). Bonhoeffer notes that we never ask this question in our day unless we have grasped "God's judgment over humankind and his grace in the cross of Jesus Christ" (511). Having recognized his weakness, the young man turns to God's Word, for only God "is a match for sin" (512). He has proven a match for sin "in Jesus Christ by forgiving us all our sins (cf. John 15:3!); he still does it by letting us know his word of grace and of judgment and by judging and being merciful to us with every new day" (512). Therefore, when under trial and temptation the believer must go "to God's word alone," which is the way to walk the blameless path (512).

According to Psalm 119:10, desiring the blameless way by turning to God's Word invites seeking with a whole heart and also praying for steadfastness in God's commandments. God's Word will always lead one to God: "Whoever has received God's word must begin to seek God; he can do nothing else" (512). Those who receive God's Word desire more and more of God, and God obliges, for he desires "to be fully glorified in us and be revealed in his full abundance" (513). This seeking will be a life-long task of learning from the Bible, for "this word is alive and inexhaustible, for God himself lives in it" (513).

We need not worry that the Word will not be enough for us; we need only worry about straying from God's Word (513). To this end, Psalm 119:11 mentions treasuring the Word in one's heart to avoid sinning against God. Bonhoeffer argues that it is not enough to have the Word in one's mind. The Word must be savored in one's heart, "just as the word of a beloved person dwells in our heart, even when we do not think about it consciously" (514). This description of treasuring the Word in the heart is very close to what Bonhoeffer wished his students to do in the time of meditation after a morning service. He claims:

> Therefore, it is never enough to have read God's word. It must enter us deeply, dwell in us like the Holiest of Holies in the sanctuary, so that we do not stray in thoughts, words, and deed. Often it is better to read little and slowly in the Scriptures, and to wait until it has penetrated into us, than to know much about God's word but not to "treasure" it. (514)

At this point Bonhoeffer begins to highlight another one of his favorite themes, the joy one has in following God's path. Treasuring God's Word naturally leads to thanking God for teaching us his Word (Ps. 119:12) and to teaching others what we have learned (119:13). The path of the faithful must include such praise (514) and must do the difficult work of expressing with the lips what is known in the mind and treasured in the heart (515). Without such rejoicing "there is no walking in the way of God" (515; see 119:14).

This is true because "God's word creates joy in the one who takes it in. It is the joy about the fellowship with God that has been given once again. It is the joy about the redemption from fear and sin. It is the joy of the one who has lost his way and after a long night found the right way once again" (515–16). God's Word gives joy because God is the source of all joy. So, "Where the word of God is, there is joy. . . . God's word is the source of all joy, and the paths of his witnesses are full of such joy because they are the paths that God himself has walked and still walks with us" (516). Those who follow Jesus know this joy, but those who do not cannot know the joy that comes from the cross and the resurrection (517).

In 119:15–16 the psalmist promises to meditate on God's precepts, keep his eyes focused on God's ways, delight in God's statutes, and remember God's Word. These pledges prompt Bonhoeffer to reflect on his convictions about meditation, exegesis, and developing a biblical memory in which he participates in the biblical story, ideas he expressed in *Life Together*. Concerning meditation Bonhoeffer confesses, "I need time for God's word and often have to ponder the words for a long time in order to understand the precepts of God correctly" (517). As he ponders these words, treasuring them in his heart, he seeks God's Word, God's direction for each new day: "God's word is not the sum of a few general sentences that could be in my mind at any time; rather it is God's daily new word addressed to me, expounded in its never-ending wealth of interpretation" (517). Those who want God's words, not their own, must soak in the Word (517).

But to soak in this Word one must engage in exegesis, in careful biblical interpretation. Recall that Bonhoeffer made his students examine New Testament concepts from the Greek New Testament. One needs exegesis "to recognize and understand God's word in Scripture as God's word" (517). Bonhoeffer does not favor skimming the surface of a passage to find an application that may or may not come from the actual context of that passage. He does not approve of finding applications from a passage that do not come naturally from the words, sentences, concepts, and theology of that passage. Yet exegesis alone is not enough. One must "take God's word prayerfully" into the heart (517). One must listen and obey it. Therefore, as for exegesis and meditation, "The one does not exist without the other. But both are reflection, which needs to be practiced on a daily basis" (517). Both are needed to find and stay on God's path, and God's path alone (518).

They are also the means by which one develops a personal, formative biblical memory. One forgets with one's whole being, and one remembers with one's whole being (518). Constant attention to the Word of God, then, requires embedding the Bible's narratives, poems, and epistles in our minds and hearts until they become part of us. This is why Bonhoeffer argued in *Life Together* for readings from longer sections of the whole Bible in community worship. Once the whole Bible becomes part of us, we will love it, and "only love protects us from forgetting" (518). Yet even love needs repetition to remain vibrant. Bonhoeffer adds, "Faith and Obedience live out of remembrance and repetition. Remembrance becomes the power of the present because it is the living God who has acted for me once and assures me of that today" (518). By "remembrance" Bonhoeffer means embodied memory, for "in and of itself the past is irrelevant. But because something decisive happened 'for me' in the past, the past becomes present for the one who grasps the 'for me' in faith" (518). The one who lives with such awareness is able to grasp what remembering Jesus daily truly means (519).

Bonhoeffer's last section covers Psalm 119:17–21 before breaking mid-sentence. His overall theme is "opened eyes," which he takes from verse 18. Opened eyes come from God, the giver of life. In verse 17 the psalmist asks that God deal bountifully with him so that he may live and observe God's Word. As in his comments on 119:1, Bonhoeffer stresses the concrete goodness of life here. Life is not just an idea, an abstract goal. Ideas exist for life, not the other way round (519). Life from God comes from his Word, and his Word affirms life now, not just life after death. Bonhoeffer claims,

"God's word is not in the hereafter; it does not lower life to a means to an end; rather, it protects life from succumbing to the contradiction, to the lordship of ideas" (519). Life now and life after death are parts of a single whole, so praying for life's needs and joys now is not a betrayal of God's Word. It is an affirmation of it (520).

Only opened eyes see the wonders of God's world and God's Word (Ps. 119:18). Once again Bonhoeffer desires more than illumination of the mind. Each day he longs to have God awaken his heart so that he may see in God's Word what God has in store for the new day (520). When God opens one's eyes in this manner, all sorts of issues get solved. As Bonhoeffer explains, "What had appeared dead to me is full of life; contradictions resolve themselves into a higher unity; harsh demands become gracious commands. Within the human word I hear God's eternal word; in past history I recognize the present God and his working for my salvation" (521). All these resolutions are ultimately possible because of God's revelation in Jesus Christ, who unites God's Word: "Through him, the word receives life, contradictions receive unity, revealed things unfathomable depth. Lord, open my eyes" (521).

The last three verses that Bonhoeffer discusses focus on the believer's guest status on earth (Ps. 119:19), longing for obedience (119:20), and assurance that God judges the arrogant (119:21). Though I may read future events in Bonhoeffer's life into his comments, they seem more autobiographical than what precedes them. At the very least, they describe his situation in Sigurdshof, as he keeps walking the path he believes God has called him to pursue.

Bonhoeffer knows that he has been a guest on earth, because God encountered him and opened his eyes. In this way he follows in the footsteps of the Bible's great saints featured in Hebrews 11, at least in the sense that they were strangers and pilgrims on earth (521). In one of his most moving statements in these meditations he comments on what his guest status means. It means he has a house and possessions, but not that he has anyone to stand up for him when he suffers violence and oppression (522). It means that the earth has a right to his work and strength, but not that he can despise the earth (522). It means that he has a permanent home with God, but, he adds, "I may not evade my destiny to be a guest and a stranger, and thereby God's call into this sojourner status, by dreaming away my earthly life with thoughts about heaven. There is a very godless homesickness for the other world that will certainly not be stilled by a homecoming" (522). It means embracing the role of a guest, yet realizing that "because I am nothing on earth but a guest, without rights, without support, without security, because God himself has made me so weak and lowly, therefore, he has given me one single pledge for my goal: his word" (522). It means, then, "Wherever the word of home is with me, I will find my way in the strange land; I will find my rights in the midst of injustice, my support in the midst of insecurity, my strength in my work, patience in the midst of suffering" (522). The guest has from God what he needs. The guest can thus be at home anywhere in God's creation.

Since the guest depends on God for all these things, feeling that God's Word is hidden is a great trial, perhaps the greatest (523). Any form of confusion hurts, as Bonhoeffer learned in his trip to the United States, and as many of his students and colleagues discovered in the legalization controversy. So Bonhoeffer fears falling back on his own principles when God's Word seems obscure to him. He knows that God's Word is consistent; it is "not one thing today and another tomorrow" (523). God does not give words that make no sense, so Bonhoeffer does not fear this. He fears following his own ways instead of God's. He fears treating his life as some special case when God's will is generally very clear, when his greatest problem is not *doing* God's will instead of not *knowing* God's will (524).

Bonhoeffer had not only learned from his seminary work and its attendant journeying that he was a guest on earth. He had also learned through them what it meant to long to be obedient to God. In Psalm 119:20 the psalmist describes himself as crushed by the longing to fulfill God's demands as he lives as a guest, a stranger on earth. He feels the pressure of accepting that he may have no human advocate on earth, that God's demands take precedence over all solely human concerns (525). He wants very badly to do God's will.

Bonhoeffer states that the weight of this desire is so heavy that fervent piety is not enough to keep him following God's path as a guest in a harsh world. After all, such fervor is temporary. More is needed. Therefore, Bonhoeffer asserts, "The longing for God's word is distinguished, not by the heat of piety, but by perseverance to the Word until the end" (525). This means that true longing to obey stands and stays because God never leaves or forsakes his people. True longing seeks "God where intellect and experience reject him" and calls on him even "when all strength sinks in death," when God will not release the believer from his path (525).

All this commitment could seem to be nothing more than belief in a lost cause if God did not judge the haughty, but Psalm 119:21 declares "accursed" those too arrogant to turn to God. Bonhoeffer defines "the haughty" as "those who are self-satisfied, who do not heed divine and human right, for whom mercy means nothing, the despisers of the word of God and of the faithful. Haughtiness before God is the root of all disobedience, of all violence, of all thoughtlessness" (526). God stands with the weak and humble, however things may look at the moment. The gospel includes the fact that "God's sword" looms "over the haughty of this earth," and the community of faith can see bits of this judgment "as the haughty fall and perish, even in this time" (526). The church cannot take much joy in this judgment, however, for "together with the haughty, innocents perish" (526). This leaves the church believing God's promise that evil will not always triumph, and knowing that this word of warning is for them as well (526).

The handwritten text ends at this point, but one can sense that Bonhoeffer is again committed to the path he thinks God has chosen for him. His confidence in God—God's Word, God's call, and God's crucified and risen Son, Jesus Christ—allow him to continue in his theological work at the seminary on behalf of the Confessing Church. As he states in a Sigurdshof sermon on 1 Corinthians 15:54 ("Death is swallowed up in victory"), dated November 26, 1939, he has this confidence "against the graves of our loved ones, against the dying nature outside, against the death that the war casts over us once again. We see the reign of death, but we preach and believe in the victory of Jesus Christ over death" (478–88). This is the basis for "perseverance to the Word until the end" (525).

On March 15, 1940, Bonhoeffer, Bethge, and the students finished the term and left Sigurdshof. Three days later the Gestapo came and sealed the building as they had done at Finkenwalde. There was no way to continue the work, and that was a terrible loss to the Confessing Church and to Bonhoeffer as well. But Bonhoeffer had learned by now the truth of what he had declared in his October 26, 1938, lecture on the path of the Confessing Church and the legalization controversy. He had learned that only God knows the next step on one's path, so we live by faith, not by sight, as far as the future goes. He was also learning that perseverance to the end is what God asks, and that faithfulness equals success in God's eyes. Thus, returning to Sigurdshof and Köslin in 1939 proved to his colleagues, to his students and former students, and to Bonhoeffer himself, as it also proves to us, that those who believe obey, and those who obey believe.

Observations for Incarnational Seminaries Today

Some seminary teachers, students, and alumni today experience close parallels between their situations and Bonhoeffer's. There are many places in the world today where Christianity and training for Christian ministry are suppressed, at times brutally. For most of us, though, learning from Bonhoeffer's seminary experiences from 1937–1940 is a matter of comparing a greater level of difficulty to our lesser ones. Regardless of our situation, this era in his life suggests attention to at least three points that remain crucial to personal seminary ministry.

Ministry to Former Students

First, Bonhoeffer's work and writings during this period highlight the importance of encouraging former students in their current ministries. Incarnational seminaries do not simply give their graduates certificates and diplomas and send them off with good wishes and contact information for the development office. They continue to offer resources and face-to-face counsel for improved ministry, and they visit the lonely. From close contact with graduates in their churches, incarnational seminaries also have the privilege of learning how to prepare future generations of pastors.

This ministry of encouragement involves helping alumni with current and continuous pastoral issues, such as evangelism, catechizing children, spiritual counseling, and preaching. The retreat at Zingst in June 1938 with former students covered such matters. It also includes helping former students stand against temptations to make unbiblical compromises. Bonhoeffer's exhortations during the legalization controversy provide an example of this type of ministry. Several letters to Bonhoeffer from students and others at this time reveal that though unfettered ministry was a real consideration for many thinking about legalization, the harsh truth was that status and money played large roles as well. So did personal safety. Bonhoeffer and others urged their brothers and sisters in the Confessing Church to put confession of biblical truth and separation from heresy above financial and professional concerns, even in difficult circumstances.

To be frank, like the seminary, most graduates will often face temptations related to financial issues and status. Faithfulness to a serious, biblical path in a money-driven and celebrity-oriented culture will always be hard. This ministry of encouragement may also include ministry to persons who have already made such compromises. Bonhoeffer reached out to those who decided to become legalized. By the time most of his students were soldiers, he was very understanding about pressures that placed them in compromising situations.

Perseverance in Incarnational Education

Second, sustaining personal seminary education often requires sacrificial perseverance by faculty, students, church leaders, and supporters. Many faculty members reflect Bonhoeffer's commitment in their own ways and their own settings. They are often underpaid and have to supplement their incomes with pastoral work or teaching extra classes to make ends meet. Others are paid sufficiently, but they labor in teaching, writing, preaching, and denominational efforts to the extent that they are weary and in danger of poor health. Many administrators carry massive burdens related to finding donors, meeting constituent demands, dealing with new generations of students, treating faculty and staff members well, and keeping focused on the purpose for which the institution exists. Some trustees and supporters do their best to provide the wisdom and funding the seminary needs. More than a few students balance work, study, home, and ministry. They have not entered seminary lightly and intend to learn and be formed into persons who can begin well in ministry.

Hebrews 10:35–36 reads: "Therefore do not throw away your confidence, which has a great reward. For you have need of endurance, so that when you have done the will of God you may receive what is promised." The whole Bible makes these same points over and over again in a variety of ways. So do Bonhoeffer's writings from 1937–1940. They indicate the toll perseverance in hard seminary work can take. They provide theological reasons for staying the course, and they reveal Bonhoeffer's desire to escape the realities his ministry involved. They reveal some reasons he kept walking the path and demonstrate to us that we can do the same.

Providing a Visible Witness of Faithfulness

Third, the seminary that perseveres in incarnational ministry offers a visible testimony of the importance of ministerial preparation as one of the acts of Christ's body. This witness heartens others already in the same work. It likewise gives hope to those thinking of beginning such work. Most importantly it lives out the theology of the personal gospel shared by disciples with others who will pass on the faith. It embraces ministry to people, who will share eternity with their teachers.

Many of us take comfort in notes, cards, letters, and e-mails from former students thanking us for our ministry in their lives. I find many of the letters Bonhoeffer received from his students encouraging as well. Their gratitude for what he had done for them and gratitude that he was spared to continue the work are equally touching. Thus, these letters provide a living tangible witness to how others respond to incarnational ministry.

Conclusion

Weariness is a natural part of life, and, as an old saying goes, it makes cowards of us all at times. There is no benefit in acting as if such is not the case. Awareness of the struggle to maintain quality incarnational education is part of the battle. The immediate future is likely to be hard on seminary education that tries to form students academically, spiritually, and personally. I suspect that only those who have decided to endure will have the purpose and focus to do so. Yet if we think it is the most theologically viable type of ministerial formation, we must not doubt the priority of incarnational education and accept that lesser work is all we can accomplish. New and old methods will be needed, and we must strive to adapt and adopt these. But we will not focus on such difficult solutions if we default on our commitment.

6

Life Together Today

Some Possibilities for Incarnational Seminaries

God does not want the word to be proclaimed by pho-
nograph records, but rather by witnesses.

Dietrich Bonhoeffer (1936)

Introduction

Bonhoeffer moved on to new communities after he left Sigurdshof.
Later in 1940 he spent time in a monastery where he began to write
what he hoped would be a thorough work on ethics and where,
much to his delight, he heard the monks read portions of *Life Together* aloud. As most readers of this book will know, however,
after March 1940 his chief community outside his family, closest
friends, and his fiancée became those with whom he was involved
in the Resistance. With these determined people he found new ways
to exercise what he believed was concrete obedience to Christ in
the absence of his public ministry, which the government had taken
away. He might have pursued this path regardless of what happened to his seminary work. We cannot know for certain. But we

are certain he died as a Christian member of the Resistance, thereby leaving a complicated and disputed legacy.

We can also be certain that he left a legacy of determined commitment to incarnational seminary education. His vision of theological education was not simply informational or formational. It was both. He did not believe in giving up academic or formational rigor. His desire to build more faithful churches was inextricably linked to his view of the personal shaping of pastors. He sought to prepare witnesses sent by Jesus.

Now over six decades have passed since Bonhoeffer left Sigurdshof. It is fair to ask what parts of his theology and practices of seminary ministry are transferable to our work today. I have stated several applications from his writings in previous chapters, and I will not rehearse those here. Instead, in this chapter I will argue that Bonhoeffer's theology of embodied seminary education remains valid despite some objections to this position, I will note various ways of being faithful to this vision for seminary education, and I will state why seminaries that embrace this incarnational theology will have a viable ministry going forward in challenging times.

Some Objections to the Necessity of Embodied Pastoral Formation

Bonhoeffer's theological views on seminary ministry remain valid today for several reasons, as I have tried to demonstrate in the previous chapters. I will highlight three here that I think are particularly pertinent for the future of pastoral formation. First, he begins in the right place, for he starts with God's Word written, the Bible. He anchors his ideas in the Bible's treatment of Jesus's life and disciple-forming and disciple-sending patterns, as well as in the spiritual growth practices found in Psalms and other biblical books. Indeed, he could expand his theoretical base by adding texts from Proverbs and other Old Testament texts that deal with education. Second, from this biblical position he bases his methods in the core theological truth of Christ's work on our behalf; proceeds to the nature of discipleship, ministry, and the church; and only then determines what form a seminary community should take. While circumstances change, these fundamental building blocks do not. Third, he has the proper biblical goal in mind, which is to shape pastors for congregations that honor God. He rightly believes that the seminary does not only exist for its own sake. It exists to shape pastors into the good shepherds the Bible describes. These principles require persons shaping persons in face-to-face contexts.

As I have discussed the theology and practice of seminary work along these lines, conversation partners have raised certain issues. Some of these have pertained solely to economic and cultural matters, a few of which I have mentioned in previous chapters. I will not cover that ground again here. Christians must base their work in biblical theology, not in current views of what is pragmatic. When Christian work proceeds in a biblical manner, it has its best chance of succeeding in all necessary ways. Some objections have a more theological bent, and I will address briefly three that fit this category.

Epistles as a Model for Distance Education

The first issue is the connection between the Epistles and incarnational education. I have had conversations with individuals who suggest that the apostles taught people using the best distance education technology of their day, which was the epistle sent to far-flung congregations. In response, I agree that the apostles did indeed send letters, yet the letters were not like most sent today, and the recipients were not like most of today's online students.[1] The Epistles were not sent to lone individuals who then read them in private. They were addressed to individuals and congregations. They were each carried not by a government employee, but by one or more Christians sent from the apostle. These carriers were there to discuss the contents, explain the apostle's situation, and share fellowship with the recipients. Thus, these letters embodied a relationship

---

[1] I owe many of the following observations to a conversation with my colleague Frank Thielman.

already begun. Even in a letter like the one to the Romans, whom Paul had not visited yet, the apostle takes great pains to connect to the recipients through people known to both parties and through the ones bringing the letter. So one would be on firmer ground to argue that the correlation between use of electronic communication and the Epistles is one of supporting current relationships between known parties. Even then, the carrier of the letter is missing. The incarnational element is truncated at best, absent at worst.

Third John, one of the Bible's shortest epistles, speaks directly to the Epistles' very personal nature. A brief examination of the letter yields at least four relevant points. First, John knew the letter's recipients very well. He uses an array of personal terms in the epistle. He calls Gaius "beloved" in verse 1. He mentions "the brothers," which more than likely means "brothers and sisters," three times (vv. 3, 5, and 10), and rejoices that "my children are walking in the truth" in verse 4. He closes with two mentions of "friends" in verse 15, asking that each one be greeted "by name." All these terms denote intimate existing personal relationships. Second, John uses the letter to deal with a particular problem caused by two men he calls by name (vv. 9–12). Even his rebukes are personal. Third, he states his preference for direct speech and contact with them. In verses 13–14 he writes, "I had much to write to you, but I would rather not write them with pen and ink. I hope to see you soon, and we will talk face to face." He pens similar things in 2 John 12. This brief epistle demonstrates, then, the utterly personal nature of an epistle and an apostolic desire to do on earth what believers expect to do in the new heavens and earth, have face-to-face contact.

Body-of-Christ Terminology and Seminaries

The second issue is the suitability of using body-of-Christ language to describe a seminary. It is important to state unequivocally that a seminary is not a church, whatever one's church polity. Nevertheless, a seminary is a ministry of the body of Christ as believers use their spiritual gifts to minister to and with other believers. If it is not such an operation of the body of Christ, it should not be preparing pastors.

Put another way, Protestant churches typically argue that the church is a body of faithful men and women in which the Word of God is preached and the sacraments are rightly administered. The very idea that one can determine if the sacraments have been rightly administered requires in part asking how the body of Christ has been behaving outside the confines of the church gathering. Church discipline implies that body life occurs in the communities and families in which we live and in the vocations we exercise to God's glory. It seems to me appropriate, then, to ask how believers engaged in seminary work fulfill the biblical standards for the body of Christ in that work and how they treat others while doing so.

One does not have to equate a seminary and a church, or a family and a church for that matter, to apply the principle of Christ's body to it. Bonhoeffer takes the argument further, of course, for he defines the church as existing where the Word is preached, the sacraments are duly administered, and the ministry gifts of the people operate in daily life. Each of the three characteristics requires a visible, physical presence. Regardless, the point is the same: body language is appropriate for the work of believers in the world.

Missions and Incarnational Education

The third issue is that stressing face-to-face education may inhibit world missions. In personal conversations some people have stated to me that there are insufficient numbers of teachers and seminaries in many developing nations. The solution, they believe, is to utilize online means of education. Others add that there are also isolated places in countries like the United States and Australia that have no seminaries. Thus, a mission mandate requires online education, not just extension teaching. Beginning with this mission mandate, however, many seminaries then include students who have extensive access to teachers and other student colleagues.

This argument certainly begins with good motives. Nonetheless, it has some practical and theological flaws. One of the most practical issues is that many developing nations have no reliable Internet connection and few funds for computers. Some also have oppressive governments able to block and monitor Internet classes. These places will need other means of help. They still need human teachers for small and large groups. I agree that online classes should be used if no personal means are currently available locally. But capable persons must be deployed as soon as possible afterward. Regardless, the existence of emergency cases hardly justifies offering online classes to people in no emergency whatsoever. Seminaries could indeed offer online instruction only in emergency cases, but they should not posit missions as a reason for impersonal education when their real goal (or at least the actual result) is to enroll local students to increase tuition revenues.

As for the theological basis of missions, I cannot help but return to God's model. He sent the prophets. He sent his Son, Jesus. His Son spent much of his ministry training a small number of disciples in a face-to-face manner. Jesus sent the people he trained. They evangelized and equipped others, and the gospel expanded to the ends of the earth in a few decades. The personal, organic way of ministry hurtled the church forward. We have no guarantees about numerical growth when exercising biblical ministry, but by any standard of measure this incarnational method remains successful. Shaping people for service is God's means of developing believers in friendships, marriages, churches, and communities. Frankly, this method seems slow to some of us. It requires patience. It does not follow an industrial model. Media can supplement this effort, as epistles did, but seeking other methods simply replaces a biblical model for a lesser one. The longer we seek to find ways around the biblical model, the more time we waste.

Varied Means of Faithful Incarnational Pastoral Formation

Bonhoeffer was an educational reformer. He was already worried that universities and seminaries were not shaping true disciples of

Jesus before the Nazis took power in 1933. Thus, his seminaries employed the specific practices described in *Life Together* to attempt to reach the biblical goals for ministers set forth in *The Cost of Discipleship*. Each practice can be traced back to the ultimate goal of shaping messengers sent from Jesus to shepherd his people, the body of Christ. Intentionality is evident. Bonhoeffer recognized that other communities could use the suggested practices as they deemed appropriate. For example, he knew that life together is different when spouses and children are involved. Thus, he thought there was inherent flexibility in his approach. I believe he was correct, since I have seen seminaries in many nations using similar practices. As I stated in chapter 2, Bonhoeffer's methods are not unique. Since they are still used to some degree in several places, I will simply suggest how they might apply in five possible venues.

Large Seminaries

Large seminaries present a particular set of problems to personal approaches to pastoral formation. They may have lots of students in various programs with faculty members teaching numerous subjects. They usually have lots of different class schedules operating at once. Students cannot know all other students, and frankly all faculty members cannot know all their colleagues. Many Christian colleges face similar challenges in trying to produce spiritually formed graduates.

I do not believe these problems are insuperable if the institution considers incarnational education a priority. These seminaries usually have chapel services, and attendance could be expected of all students and faculty. If the seminary is too large for everyone to attend, then services can be held at more than one time in more than one place. A seminary with several faculty members and hundreds of students should have sufficient preachers and worship leaders.

Worshiping in community binds people together and gives them a vision for ministering to one another and to persons outside the community. It gives people the chance to pray for one another. Thus, it provides venues for fellowship that help integrate faith, learning, and service. The student body can be divided into mentoring groups that meet regularly and are led by faculty, staff, and senior students. Night classes could be enriched by some time of common worship, no doubt shorter in duration than regular chapel, though one could argue that chapel services do not need to last an hour or more to meet the community's needs. Fellowship meals and activities can happen in seminary housing blocks. Frankly, simply scheduling a few minutes for Bible reading, prayer, and personal conversation would be an improvement in many instances, as would the seminary's being committed to smaller class sizes.

The structural key, I believe, is for these seminaries to examine, for example, how Oxford has colleges within the whole university, and how some universities separate students into colleges. They should look at how Christian universities sometimes divide their student body by schools and have special chapel services, and how these colleges enhance spiritual life on and off campus in large and small groups. They should see how large, diverse Christian universities provide a range of smaller spiritual development opportunities. Good examples exist. Most of all, once incarnational education becomes a priority, the community should talk about *how* they will get this priority fulfilled, not *whether* they will do so. They can then see how common worship, common work, and common perseverance can occur. Good people tend to find the way forward, and large seminaries have good people. But they will need the vision and the freedom to do the right thing.

Small Seminaries

Smaller seminaries have their own set of challenges. In my experience the biggest challenge is the fact that they have fewer people doing more things. But they have the advantage of a student body small enough that most students and faculty can know one another. At Beeson Divinity School (c. 150 students) we have chapel only once a week, but all students, faculty, and staff members are expected to attend, and care is taken to make this a significant experience. Students agree to attend when they are accepted into the community. A community lunch follows chapel. Students, faculty, staff, family members, university personnel, and city community members attend. Every full-time student agrees to be part of a mentoring group that meets for an hour once a week. A faculty member convenes these groups, and I would also be happy to have senior students, who, after all, are hoping to be in pastoral settings soon, to lead as well. Prayer and fellowship are the main goals, and faculty members have discretion in how they wish to handle the time. We could do more to facilitate daily spiritual discipline.

Other small seminaries have similar practices. When I was a faculty member at Trinity Episcopal School for Ministry, there were daily Morning Prayer (thirty minutes), a weekly communion service, and mentoring groups. We assessed every student's spiritual development every year. Most students lived in the community. In contrast, Trinity Theological College (c. 60–80 students) in Perth, Western Australia, offers most of its classes in a once-a-week format. It owns no housing. My friends there have chapel each day classes meet for about thirty minutes to allow full- and part-time students the opportunity to be part of a worshiping community. They also have mentoring groups. Again, there are many ways to achieve face-to-face formation, and good people find the best ways to achieve this goal in their own settings.

Seminary Enrichment Programs

Bonhoeffer's specific practices could be carried out in special programs run by one or more seminaries. For instance, a seminary could make a semester-long Finkenwalde seminary experience count as part of the credits needed for a degree or certificate. This could involve men and women living at or near a site and agreeing to be part of morning and evening worship, meditation, and significant classes. Seminaries with housing for students on campus may have the best chance to make such programs feasible. Work could be done on site or in the community. Persons who have graduated from a seminary with an MDiv or an MA could also wish to have this sort of community experience, and people who have done their degrees completely online may also want this experience, and certainly need it. Short-term courses offered in summer and January terms, or even in a retreat setting, could provide a starting place for proposed longer programs.

The main keys are to have good faculty members, prepared and engaged students, and a welcoming site conducive to reflection, not noise, yet able to provide opportunities for interaction with the community around the site. Along these lines, it may be worthwhile to recall that Finkenwalde, Köslin, Gross Schlönwitz, and Sigurdshof were either small towns or rural areas. Such places are cheaper to operate in these days, so they may be more viable than a site in a city.

What characteristics do the faculty and staff members who serve in such programs share? They are committed to face-to-face academic and formational instruction that gives students models and colleagues. They are committed to preserving as much community life as possible, believing this is the best way to shape persons who will be *serving* in Christian faith communities. They are committed to life under God's Word, and thus to common worship, common prayer, serious study, and the growth of individuals within the community. While they recognize the importance of communicating life-changing information, they adhere equally to the importance of people helping one another become serious shepherds for God's people. They do not choose between rigorous thought and rigorous practice. They insist on both. Most importantly, they are convinced that the Bible directs them on this path, however hard it may be.

University Theology Department Enrichment Programs

Since some Christian universities offer BA, MA, and PhD degrees, it is feasible for them to add or incorporate Bonhoeffer's ideas into these academic programs. Students taking the MA and PhD programs often enter church, college, and seminary ministries, and do so without weighty instruction in pastoral ministry or spiritual formation of the type Bonhoeffer's seminaries modeled. For such persons it seems reasonable to offer a version of the programs just described in the suggestions for seminary enrichment programs. It also seems reasonable to require accepted and funded Christian MA and PhD students preparing to teach theological subjects to begin the day in worship, to receive some teaching in pastoral work, and to do some teaching in churches as a portion of their program.

Even if these students never enter paid church ministry, their participation in local churches will probably improve. The skills they gain will also aid them in collegial relationships, student advising, supporting local churches, and building up local communities where they teach. Faith and learning will be integrated more readily. Bonhoeffer would have benefitted from such experiences when he was a student.

Church-Based Internship Programs

I expect that church-based internship programs will flourish in the coming generation. If seminaries continue on their current impersonal path, and if online programs fail to deliver what is needed in the way I think they will fail, small local forms of pastoral training will emerge. Of course, many internship programs already exist. Many of these are like Bonhoeffer's seminaries in that they are a year or less in length, they enroll small numbers of people, they expect interns to possess at least one theological degree, they include some academic work and some practical church work, and they connect interns to a local community of faith.

These programs usually have specific strengths and weaknesses. The weaknesses are that they struggle to provide the sort of extensive academic content a seminary faculty can offer. They are dependent on the funding an individual congregation can muster. They are not able to take large numbers of participants. The strengths are that they are not tied to accreditation programs driven by government funding requirements. They can utilize a variety of teachers as needed. They are local, practical, personal, theologically driven, and mentor-oriented. They can be combined with sister programs nearby. They may be able to help interns with housing and help keep those costs low. The best of these programs combine spiritual formation, theological analysis, and the practice of ministry. The worst of them are a means for a church to get cheap labor or for a church leader to extend his ministry brand, not invest in the ministry of others.

In the future, these programs could become very much like Bonhoeffer's seminaries. They could take in people wearied by soul-deadening liberal or conservative seminaries, and people with good theological degrees that did not include ministry practices. They could provide a community of like-minded people who can worship, pray, study, and learn to serve God's people together. They could be led by one or more full-time persons based in a local church. They could incorporate persons from other church communities too small to host their own programs. They could exist in rural, urban, or suburban settings. If these programs remain humble and flexible, they can endure for a long time. If they long to be institutions, they will likely suffer disappointment. Once again, commitment to incarnational pastoral formation will be the irreplaceable key to recovering Bonhoeffer's seminary vision.

Incarnational Seminaries and the Future

One of the most repeated reasons I have heard for moving away from personal models of education is that the future does not look good for this approach. The argument is that the world has moved to electronic devices and the flexibility they bring. This means that higher education will go this route. Doing so will cut personnel costs and eventually make education less expensive. It is as effective for conveying information as large lecture courses taught by professors the students never meet. In the meantime it will help fund traditional classes and save jobs.

I demur. No one knows the future but God, and no one but God rules the future. The world has moved toward electronic devices, but there are signs that many people want to find ways for the devices to enhance personal life, not replace it. The best use of electronic devices in education is as a potentially spectacular aid, not as a replacement. Rich people still send their kids to colleges that have personal education, and poor people line up to send their children to personal colleges like Berea (Kentucky) and College of the Ozarks (Missouri), which offer tuition remission. Large, bad, and impersonal classes at universities and seminaries do not justify impersonal classes elsewhere. And large lecture courses at universities at least allow students to meet and share with one another, as my wife recently reminded me.

Electronic classes may have some revenue value, though they also carry heavy development and delivery costs. They may have educational value, especially when taught by some of the dedicated people I know. But make no mistake, the idea is to replace these dedicated people with machines, not keep them employed. I have seen this replacement of human beings in rural America and its resulting cultural disasters, and I think there is a direct correspondence between what has happened in agriculture and what is happening in education. At this time, one has to ask how well industrial methods of containing costs have worked in education in general, in health care, and in securing employment. Regardless, God gives people responsibility and we make decisions. The future is not an inexorable force.

My demurrals aside, what matters most is that God has placed the incarnational principle at the heart of the gospel, and thus at the heart of reality. In the Old Testament the greatest person, Moses, speaks with God face-to-face. In the New Testament the greatest person, Jesus, is God speaking to people face-to-face, and he has passed that direct speaking on to the church, his body. In the Bible the human family is the nucleus of life on earth. Marriage, friendship, and worship reflect the inherently personal nature of God and his images on earth, men and women. Excellence in thought and study are evident in the Bible's diverse literary forms and profound theology. People do not change, and they will long for these relationships and for this excellence of thought as long as there are people.

Furthermore, God sends his church theologically astute pastors and teachers. These pastors are the point persons in calling their denominations, networks, and associations to sacrificial face-to-face pastoral formation, just as they are in calling them to sacrificial face-to-face evangelism and church planting. There have been hopeful signs of church renewal based on theological principles during the past several years. Biblical ministry has led to large numbers of young people becoming committed to living and sharing the gospel in global settings. Meanwhile, the revolution in world travel is at least as great as the much noticed technological revolution. We have more opportunities and means to share the gospel and form pastors in personal ways than in any other period of human history. Pastors who practice incarnational ministry in their parishes will lead the way in deploying educators as they have in sending evangelists and church planters.

Thus, incarnational seminaries have a future. They may be reborn in ways we do not yet know, but they will endure. They will require friends who believe in them, who fund them, who safeguard their excellence in study and in formation, and who persevere with those who serve in them. They will require faculty and students who seek to teach and learn from one another more than they desire a mere credential or degree. They will require persons of biblical vision. The good news is that God has always provided these people. In the end we must do the right thing, not because it will succeed as we wish, but because it is the right thing.

Conclusion

Dietrich Bonhoeffer left us many legacies of hope and faithfulness. His seminary ministry is certainly one of them. As we consider life together in the future, we can take heart from what he did in the past. One of the cruelest things the Nazis did to Bonhoeffer was to take away his seminary community. He knew it was precious; it was worth returning from America to rejoin. It was worth preserving in dark times. I like to think that his work did not end when he left Sigurdshof that cold March day. I like to think he passed it on to others who feel the same way.

General Index

Scripture Index